LIVING ALL IN

LIVING ALL IN

CHRIS
JANSSEN

*How to
Show Up for
the Life
You Want*

For you and me

"Then we will no longer be immature like children.

We won't be tossed and blown about by every
wind of new teaching.

We will not be influenced when people try to trick
us with lies so clever they sound like the truth.
Instead, we will speak the truth in love . . ."

EPHESIANS 4:14,15a

The truths that follow are my commitment to focus on
what I have, not what I've missed. What I've gained, not lost.
What I appreciate, not expect. These words are my constant
reminder that God is always for me, never against me.

And your creator is always for you as well.

CONTENTS

ACKNOWLEDGMENTS

Huge thanks to:

Scott, my husband, and our children, Nick, Chloé, and Jake, for making my life book-worthy. You are the best of my world and the reason I want to share it with others. Scott, your positive and serene spirit in all situations is contagious to me and everyone around you.

Dana and Steve Clifford, Lisa and Mark Averill, and Westgate Church in Silicon Valley, California, for being my spiritual family and raising me in the ways of Jesus. You showed me what it looks like to live all in when following God—simple, not always easy, certainly not dull, and my best bet for feeling alive.

Ivey Harrington Beckman, for giving wings to my intentions. You showed me how to put my thoughts into words, then into a keepsake for my children and a tool for my clients. You are a treasure.

Kristin Billerbeck, for making me believe I have something to say worth reading. Your writing expertise and professionalism are deeply valued.

Margaret Allen, for generously responding to my question, *I wrote a book; what's next?* You model your book *Gracious Living.*

My mom, Jackie, my dad, Larry, and my brother, Chad, for teaching me to find humor and fun in all circumstances. You are the reason I know how to love my family so well.

FOREWORD

By Steve Clifford

My granddaughter stood on the edge of our swimming pool, ready to jump into the sparkling blue water six inches below. I stood beside Colbie and assured her she could do it. My wife, Mimi, waited in the pool, arms outstretched, ready to catch Colbie when she took that first leap.

Yet Colbie remained frozen by fear and doubt. She wanted to jump. She really did. Time after time, she counted to three. And then—nothing. That edge could have been ten feet above the water instead of six inches.

In *Living All In*, my friend Chris Janssen will help you face the fears and doubts that are holding you back in life. She's a great person to guide you because she has lived this life. I've seen her face her doubts and fears—and then jump! Granted, not all those jumps were the stuff you want to post on social media. Some jumps included water up the nose or stinging eyes. Still, Chris leaped! *Living All In* is Chris giving back and guiding you with practical, intuitive coaching that shows you how to show up for the life you want and leap into it your way.

A video on my phone proves that our granddaughter faced her fear. With a bit of coaching, Colbie decided that loving arms wouldn't let her go under, so she reached back, counted to three, and jumped! Her reward? A slew of new opportunities for pool play. The world blew wide open in front of her, and Colbie has never looked back.

How about you? Are you ready to go all in with a trusted coach's guidance? True, you may get some water up your nose. And your eyes may sting a bit here and there. Chris will be there to guide you through those situations as well.

The life worth living is the life all in. A whole new world is waiting for you. *One. Two. Three. Jump!*

STEVE CLIFFORD, the senior pastor of Westgate Church in Silicon Valley, CA, from 2001 to 2022, now coaches business leaders and pastors through seminars and retreats. He is a founding board member of TBC, Transforming the Bay with Christ, *www.tbc.city*, an organization dedicated to coaching, connecting, and equipping leaders to catalyze a holistic gospel movement in the Bay Area.

LIVING ALL IN

CHAPTER 1

READY, SET, GO!

"Sometimes it is necessary to reteach a thing its loveliness,
to put a hand on its brow of the flower and retell it in words
and in touch it is lovely until it flowers again from within,
of self blessing."[1]

—GALWAY KINNELL

You are whole and ready to go. You do not need fixing because you are not broken. Celebrate that! You are right on track to show up for the life you want. Opening this book proves it.

Sure, we live in a culture that talks, writes, and sings about brokenness. It has become the social-media way to relate with others. Do you have messiness to deal with? *Everyone does.* Is your life complex? *Probably.* Have you been broken-hearted at times? *Certainly.* Are you broken? *No!* You're incredibly blessed—and your wholeness is a gift to celebrate! That wholeness is propelling you to lean forward and live your life all in.

Eleanor Roosevelt once said, "I am who I am today because of the choices I made yesterday."[2] That's life-changing truth delivered in just thirteen words!

You've made the choice to show up for the life you want, to believe in your future and the beauty of your dreams. And that choice—that brave, beautiful, effervescent choice—will make a world of difference in your life and the lives of those around you.

You've made the choice to show up for the life you want, to believe in your future and the beauty of your dreams.

OUR JOURNEY

As a life coach, I help my clients close the gap between where they are in life and where they want to be. Of all the coaching techniques I've learned, tools grounded in spiritual wisdom are the most effective. I'll use several sources of inspiration throughout *Living All In*, including Scripture, because the Bible is my source of inspiration.

I encourage you to use your chosen source of inspiration as you progress through the life truths and corresponding exercises I've included in this book. Your higher power will propel you forward as you embrace these life-changing truths as a spiritual being.

You're ready to run just as you are!

To begin our journey together, think of yourself as a runner. Think of me as your coach, getting you into position, pointing out strengths and blind spots you may not notice in yourself.

We'll move you forward faster by shouting "Ready, Set, Go!" from the starting blocks, *not behind them.* You don't need a head start to move forward, nor should you position yourself behind the blocks with a mindset of brokenness. You're ready to run just as you are! When you launch from a mindset of wholeness, you get a strong running start toward living the life you want—and this book is all about moving you in that direction. You're set to run free, my friend. You're whole and ready to go!

My favorite Bible verse is Philippians 3:13. It's packed with optimism and momentum for the future: *". . . I have not achieved it, but I focus on this one thing: Forgetting the past and looking forward to what lies ahead."* The life your higher power created you to live lies ahead, and it's time to run toward it.

THE GREAT RESET

When I was a kid, my dad was a wrestling coach. My sons, in turn, wrestled in high school. When the COVID-19 global pandemic required us to quarantine in 2020, the phrase "build your base" kept running through my mind. It's what coaches yell to their wrestlers on the mat: "Build your base! Find your center!"

You see, the strength of wrestlers originates from their core. When wrestlers get tangled up—arms and legs flailing—they must disengage, find their center, and rebuild their base.

The world came together for a colossal reset because of COVID-19. It was painful for sure—lots of flailing! For me, this interruption was a reminder to find my center and check my foundation.

The one thing I know now more than ever is that I'm not in control, and my best option for a happy life is to lean into my God even more. Total surrender to my creator's plan is key to fun and freedom.

I've also learned that faithfulness, not flawlessness, is the authentic source of motivation. My clients see their best results once they, too, live all in, trusting that whatever happens in their lives

Join me in believing that progress, not perfection, is the sustainable way to live.

adds value. I want that for you too. Join me in believing that progress, not perfection, is the sustainable way to live.

Thank you for trusting me to partner with you to ignite your resourcefulness. As your coach, I'll ask questions that tap into your cleverness and creativity. You'll want to ponder those questions and write your answers in the spaces provided. Using pen and paper enhances the work by melding it into your physiology and memory.

The quarantine of 2020 taught me how small this world has become, how connected humanity really is, and how fluidly life moves when we embrace the truth that we're all in this together. We all need someone to help us get unstuck and move forward— one simple step at a time. I pray the words that follow will serve you in that way.

Your ability to attain the desires of your heart is already within you. So, we'll begin just as you are—whole and magnificent. *Ready. Set. Let's Go!*

CHAPTER 2

KNOW WHAT YOU WANT

"Our wants and longings and desires are at the core of
our identity, the wellspring from which our actions and
behavior flow. Our wants reverberate from our heart,
`the epicenter of the human person."[3]

—JAMES K.A. SMITH

What do you want? If you're stumbling to answer that
question, imagine how far you will go when you do know!
A stellar starting place for self-work is understanding what
you want and where you want to go.

Martha Beck, the best-selling author of *Finding Your Own North
Star*, tells us, "People who get what they want tend to be the ones
who make the effort to *know* what they want."[4] As your coach, my
goal is to help you lock onto your North Star and move in that
direction with confidence and enthusiasm.

An off-the-blocks way to discover what you want is to state
what you don't want. What you want is often at the opposite end

of what you don't! So, take a moment and ask yourself, *"What do I absolutely NOT want?"* Write your answer here:

> *To become old and useless!*

Answering this question isn't about focusing on what you don't want. It's about recognizing it just long enough to ignite your ingenuity to pivot 180 degrees.

So, what's the polar opposite of what you don't want? That isn't a problem-solving question because I don't solve problems for people. I'm here to help you tap into yourself—to get you curious about what you want and what works for you. To help you speak and act for yourself. I want you to get what you want!

Ask yourself the following questions with a 180-degree mindset pivot (and what you don't want behind you). Your response may be a rough sketch; fine-tuning will come later. For now, get on paper what has been waving at you from your soul, striving to get your attention!

What do I see as my future? What do I want?

> *To be useful and needed and purposeful and effective.*

Doesn't it feel great to see what you want on paper? Celebrate that! Putting your dream in writing is a huge first step toward showing up for the life you want.

LEAPING OVER HURDLES

Here's a next-step question to ask yourself, especially if you think hurdles impede your path to getting what you want: *If life were different, and I already had what I most wanted, how would I know life was different? What would I notice?*

Putting your dream in writing is a huge first step toward showing up for the life you want.

When my client, Tina, answered this question, here's how the conversation unfolded:

Tina: I would know life was different because winning the lottery made me wealthy, so I'd notice I was happy.

Me: Great! Describe your happiness.

Tina: I'd have options.

Me: Describe options.

Tina: I'd have the option to do what I love instead of working at my current bank job.

Me: Super! What do you love?

Tina: Fitness, especially yoga.

Me: So, what does doing what you love look like?

Tina: Owning a yoga studio.

Me: Do you have to win the lottery to own a yoga studio?

Tina: Yes, because I don't have the funds to quit my job and start a studio.

Me: Is that true? Is winning the lottery the only way you can open a yoga studio, or are there other options?

Tina: There are other ways. Actually, I've saved enough to qualify for a loan.

Me: Fantastic! (Tina proceeded to tell me the logistics of how she could make this career change happen within the year.)

Me: So, Tina, what do you want?

Tina: To open my yoga studio!

Me: And how does knowing you have the option to do that make you feel?

Tina: Happy!

Take time to get creative and truthful with yourself about what you want and what's hindering you from getting it.

What Tina wanted was a career that embraced her love of fitness. What hindered her turned out to be a false belief that an event beyond her control, such as winning the lottery, was her only option for happiness.

Even if Tina hadn't saved the funds to secure a small business loan, she still figured out that what she wanted was a career shift, not a lottery win. Tina had options to strategize toward the life she wanted. She had the power to leap over hurdles.

Take time to get creative and truthful with yourself about what you want and what's hindering you from getting it. Ask yourself the following questions. They will limber your mind and spirit—and your answers will reveal a lot about what's real and what's not.

What's hindering me from getting what I want?

_____

_____

Is what's hindering me real or merely perceived?

_____

_____

Did someone else convince me that this hurdle is standing in my way? If so, whom? Why did I believe that individual?

_____

_____

If I face a true hurdle, what's another way to get what I want?

> *Make a plan.*
> *Have goals*

Can I go around the hurdle?

> *Maybe not*

Is it possible that hurdle is the way forward?

How do you feel after answering those questions? I hope you feel empowered because you are! Recognizing what's blocking you enables you to leap with a clear perspective that propels you up and over.

In the following chapter, we'll talk about old labels stuck to you like wrinkled name tags—and how they may be muddling your story. What you've been telling yourself (perhaps for years) may be the hurdles keeping you from knowing who you are and getting what you want.

CHAPTER 3

CHECK YOUR LABELS

"And now I'm going to tell you who you are, really are . . ."

—JESUS TO PETER (MATTHEW 16:18 MSG)

When clients ask me to help them find themselves, my response is usually, "Stop looking for your identity. Create it instead!"

So, who are you? Do you know yourself? Are you in touch with authentic you? Awareness of yourself involves being conscious of all the dynamic and unique characteristics that make up who you are. If you want to show up for the life you want, you must know who you are—the true-blue you. (Not who you pretend to be. Not who others say you are or want you to be.)

You can't find what isn't lost, and your identity isn't lost, my friend! It's right there in the DNA your creator gave you, waiting for you to make it a reality. Life isn't about finding yourself. It's about knowing yourself, then creating the life you want to live. Only you get to create the life that reflects the extraordinary person your creator imprinted on your soul.

> *Life isn't about finding yourself. It's about knowing yourself, then creating the life you want to live.*

STUCK ON YOU

Getting in touch with the true you is freeing because many labels may be sticking to you, like wrinkled name tags. And those labels are talking all the time, saying things to you and those around you.

Labels are tricky things, embarrassing sometimes. If you've ever forgotten to remove your name tag after an event and walked through the rest of your day wearing it here, there, and everywhere, you know the eye-roll feeling when you discover that you were tagged all day. And you also know how good it feels to peel off that label and toss it in a trash can.

(Hang on to that done-with-it feeling because we'll return to it.)

Some labels can keep you glued to a life you don't want. You've probably been collecting a few of those for years. Some you stuck on yourself: *"I'm shy." "I'm over-sensitive." "I'm too introverted." "I talk too much." "I'm the victim here." "I won't ever have _____." "I suffer from _____." "I can't _____."*

Perhaps a few labels were plastered on you by people close to you: *"You don't measure up!" "You need to act more like your sister."*

And some labels are glued to your back—and you have no idea how they got there: *"Such a disappointment!" "Not enough!" "Unlovable!"*

Labels like those are trash—way wrong, causing confusion and harm. And yet, they stick around.

On the other hand, some labels are stellar, accurate, and helpful for living all in. You'll want to recognize these gems: *"I'm a work in progress and a masterpiece simultaneously." "I'm resourceful." "I'm equipped." "I'm able." "I'm the perfect person for the task at hand." "I'm beautifully and wonderfully made." "I'm lovable." "I'm more than enough." "I'm a gift."*

Whatever the source of the labels stuck on you, it's time to trash the unhealthy ones so you can celebrate the wonderful ones and create the identity you want—the true you!

MANAGING LABELS

To help you recognize your sticky labels, here's one that landed on me in my younger days via well-meaning teachers, coaches, and loved ones: *over-sensitive*. I often heard, "Don't be so sensitive, Chris!" "Get over it." "Toughen up!"

As a young person, my inability not to "be so sensitive" became a second problem on top of being sensitive, which I used to think was wrong. I looked for ways to numb the feeling of inadequacy the "over-sensitive" label gave me—as if I were *less than* because I felt things deeply. I tried various numbing potions as a young person: food, excessive exercise, and alcohol. These potions were solutions—until they weren't.

> *Whatever the source of the labels stuck on you, it's time to trash the unhealthy ones so you can celebrate the wonderful ones and create the identity you want— the true you!*

In 1991, when I graduated from college, clinical psychologist Elaine Aron coined the term Highly Sensitive Person (HSP). Once I realized others like me were out there, I felt strengthened. (Several resources are now available on the subject should you want to learn more.)

A Highly Sensitive Person has a finely wired central nervous system and an increased awareness of physical, emotional, and social stimuli. Some HSP traits include:

- being deeply moved by beauty.
- avoiding violent movies or television shows because they feel too intense and unsettling.
- needing downtime.
- having a rich and complex inner life with deep thoughts and strong feelings.
- having a tough time receiving negative feedback.
- freezing under pressure.
- experiencing analysis paralysis.
- exhibiting high creativity.
- being detail oriented.
- having a high propensity for empathy (often having a deep empathetic and even physical response to what others think and feel).
- possessing the gift of intuition.
- being overwhelmed by sensory stimuli, such as noisy crowds, bright lights, or uncomfortable clothing. (I call this one "the Princess and the Pea Phenomenon.")

Check, check, and check! For me, knowing the HSP label exists freed my soul. I realized I wasn't inadequate, broken, or weird. I didn't need a remedy for my sensitivity. The "sensitive" label fit, and learning how to embrace it in healthy ways was a good thing!

I'm grateful for the strengths being a highly sensitive person gives me. I've learned how to manage this label well and celebrate it because my God wired me this way. A divine thumbprint on my soul says, *Chris will be a tender one for My glory!*

Managing my HSP well includes healthy acknowledgment of the positives of this label and not using it as an excuse for unproductive behavior. If I were to say to others, "I'm a highly sensitive person, so I cannot partake in this or that activity," I would become a hindrance to them and miss out on my growth. I wouldn't push myself to live outside "the Princess and the Pea" description. I would be using the HSP label as an excuse to stay inside my comfort zone.

So, that's one of my labels. Are you ready to take a look at yours?

Labels have more power than you might think because they grab your attention—and you receive what you focus on.

AN EXERCISE FOR LABEL PEELING

Labels have more power than you might think because they grab your attention—and you receive what you focus on. When spoken aloud, a label increases its power and demands even more of your focus. You may become that label without even realizing it.

Here's the good news: Now that you know unhealthy labels stick around, you can begin peeling them off! You can wad them up like an old name tag—physically, mentally, and spiritually pitching them in the trash.

On the flip side, if a label serves to move you forward and live all in, as HSP does for me, that's great! Hang on to it like a blue ribbon, especially if it helps you form an identity that aligns with what you want and reflects who you are.

Does that blue-ribbon characterization define all of you? Certainly not. However, if it's part of the authentic you, celebrate it— along with the many other characterization labels that say to you, "This is me, wonderfully made by my creator!"

When my children were little, I read Max Lucado's book, *You Are Special*, to them time and time again. I breathed Lucado's words like a prayer because he so purely communicated the beauty and wisdom of trusting in what our creator thinks about us, rather than believing the labels others try to stick on us. One line from *You Are Special* says it all:

"The more you trust my love, the less you care about their stickers."[5]

I pray that trust in the unconditional love your creator has for you will empower you to shed painful labels. Here's a soulful exercise to help you begin to embrace your true self—unfettered by unhelpful labels. The authentic you, living your vibrant identity all in.

Ask yourself two questions:

1. *What positive characterizations will I allow to stick to me to create the all-in life I want?*
2. *What negative characterizations will I peel off to create the life I want?*

Write your answers to both questions on sticky notes or name-tag stickers. Then, stick the tags all over you. Stand in front of a mirror, and peel off the answers to question two. Wad up those negative labels, and toss them in the trash.

Take the remaining stickers, and place them where you'll see them at least once in the morning and before bedtime (on your bathroom mirror, beside your nightstand, or wherever you'll notice them.) You can also take a picture of them for your smartphone or computer wallpaper.

The idea is to get the characterizations that serve you well to stick! Train your brain to believe them by reciting them aloud. This motion and emotion will anchor the identity you want—and help uncover the authentic you.

Allow awareness of your labels to spur you to act. If a label strengthens you, keep it. If it becomes a disempowering excuse, dump it. You alone get to decide how information lands on you.

There's a big difference between identifying with a label and making a label your identity.

One caution: Keep your whole self in mind. There's a big difference between identifying with a label and making a label your identity. Many remarkable features make you unique, so don't limit your identity and significance to a single part of yourself.

Remember, you get to decide how you feel. You get to choose which labels stick and which ones get peeled off and trashed. There's no wrong or right, just helpful or not. You choose.

Labels don't have the final say about you. Use them to your advantage, not your detriment. Before you call yourself a name, ask yourself if it's a name your higher power would call you. It's your divine's word that counts.

Check your labels. Check your truths. Know who you are, so you can live your life all in.

CHAPTER 4

WRITE YOUR STORY

"Everything can be taken from a man but one thing:
the last of the human freedoms—to choose one's attitude in
any given set of circumstances, to choose one's own way."[6]

—VIKTOR FRANKL, HOLOCAUST SURVIVOR

Do you have an energizing story? Or is yours an exhausting tale that's holding you back? Your story is the narrative you tell yourself, either consciously or subconsciously.

Your story interprets past, current, and future events with your life circumstances. Those circumstances don't have any meaning except those you choose to attach to them. You'll want to choose well because your subconscious (that quiet and sometimes nagging voice in your head) can pivot you from what's true if you give it free rein.

The story you tell yourself about something becomes your belief about that thing. That belief can propel you forward or hold you back. You get to choose whether you tell a story that exhausts

> *You get to choose whether you tell a story that exhausts you or one that energizes you.*

you or one that energizes you. And that story will cast shadows or light on your past, define your present, and steer your future.

Megaphone moment: *You're in charge of what you think about things!* You're fully responsible for what you declare as truth. And what you state as truth creates your story—what you believe. A thought that doesn't serve you well isn't real, unless you decide it is. You see, a belief is made up of two things: the truth and what's fabricated. It's really that simple!

I'm a sucker for cowboy stories, and I watch the hit series *Yellowstone.* When talking with his grandson, Tate, the show's leading character, John Dutton, summed up the power of re-writing one's story this way: *"You know what dreams are? It's your memories and your imagination all mixed together into this soup of what's real and what's made up. But the thing about this soup is, you can change the ingredients, Tate. You can put in whatever you want to."*[7]

So, what ingredients are in your soup? Is your story exhausting or energizing? An exhausting story is spawned when the truth and the fabricated mangle to-gether over time to create an unsound, destructive belief. You can live for years believing an exhausting story. That story may even feel comfortable and safe be-cause you've formed identity or signifi-cance in that old tale. On the flip side, an energizing story develops when the truth about an event interweaves with your positive interpretation of that truth to create a sound, constructive belief.

> You cannot control all your circumstances; you can control the meanings you choose to attach to them.

You cannot control all your circumstances; you can control the meanings you choose to attach to them. Use this jump-start exer-cise to invigorate your mind.

Think of a circumstance that led to an unwanted feeling for you. What meaning did you attach to that circumstance?

_____

_____

Was it an empowering interpretation of the event or a disempowering interpretation?

_____

If disempowering, was your interpretation of the event true or something you unintentionally fabricated?

_____

What would have been a better interpretation?

_____

_____

Now, think of a circumstance that led to a feeling you desired.

_____

_____

What meaning did you attach to that circumstance?

_____

_____

Was it an empowering interpretation of the event or a disempowering interpretation? (My guess is it was empowering.)

_____

See the difference? Controlling the meaning you attach to circumstances is a life-changing brain shift! Disempowering meanings are narratives of stories that cause despair. When natural pain happens (and it will), you get to choose if you allow the pain to crush you or roll over you like a wave. Sure, the rolling takes time, and it hurts. However, the process creates perseverance and grit for the next painful wave.

CHANGE YOUR STORY

Owning an energizing story that serves you well requires identifying and destroying the exhausting story (or stories) you've been telling yourself for days, weeks, months (or maybe years). Here's Dale's story, a client who transformed his life by changing his story.

In his twenties, Dale went to prison on drug-possession charges. Once out, he spent time in rehab for substance abuse.

Dale was clean of drugs when we first met, although his self-worth was still messy. He was also drinking heavily, out of shape, addicted to cigarettes, in an unhealthy relationship, and had settled for a job that didn't match his skill-sets and talents. At the beginning of our work together, Dale often missed sessions because he was hung over.

Dale's old story sounded like this: *I'm unworthy of what I want in life, so I deserve the negative consequences life throws at me.*

Dale, an uber-talented architect, believed he would never be good enough to succeed in his dream career. His story as a screw-up unworthy of a healthy, happy life stuck in his head.

Dale needed a new story! The assignment I gave him will help you understand how to identify your old story, so you can create a new one.

Step One: I asked Dale to create a two-column sheet of paper titled "Dale's Story." I encouraged him to write his story in the left column exactly as he heard it going through his mind. Here's what he wrote:

- I made some poor choices in my past.
- I'm a screw-up.
- I'm not enough.
- I'm not worthy of the things I want.
- I want a different job, but what's the point of interviewing; I won't get it.
- I know that I'm capable of making the amount of money I want to make, but that's just a dream. It's not real.
- Disappointment is a comfortable feeling for me.
- Not getting what I want is what I'm used to, which makes sense because people get what they deserve in life.
- I'll always make less money than others because that's how it has always been for me.

- I don't have what it takes to accomplish my dreams. Dreams are meant for other people anyway, not me.
- I'll stay at my same job.

Whew! That's an exhausting, destructive story, isn't it? Dale needed a new narrative for his life.

Step Two: To energize Dale to rewrite his story, I asked him to separate what was true and fabricated about himself by circling only the truths in his left-column list. Dale circled the following:

- I made some poor choices in my past.
- I want a different job.
- I know I'm capable of making the amount of money I want to make.
- Disappointment is a comfortable feeling for me.
- Not getting what I want is what I am used to.

Step Three: In the right column, I asked Dale to write out his new, energizing story, noting truths and new meanings.

- I made some poor choices in my past. (**truth**)
- I'll use those poor choices as my fuel to be the best friend, family member, architect, and person imaginable. I'm not my younger self; I'm now an incredible individual. I'm grateful to my past for firing me up to develop the characteristics I currently possess. (**new meaning**)
- I want a different job. (**truth**)
- I'm worthy of what I want. Because of my past, I am fiercely committed. What business wouldn't want that? A company

would be crazy *not* to hire me! (**new meaning**)

- I'm capable of making the amount of money I want to make. (**truth**)
- I will achieve what I want to in this life. (**new meaning**)
- Disappointment *was* a comfortable feeling for me. (**truth**)
- I'm energized by inspiring others to make good choices and achieve their dreams. (**new meaning**)
- I *was* used to not getting what I wanted. (**truth**)
- I know I'm worthy of what I want, and I'll achieve it. (**new meaning**)

That's an energizing, constructive story! Dale's writing his new narrative on paper was the mental jump he needed to move ahead. Sure, the positive words Dale wrote on paper took a while to transform his thinking. Some days, he took two steps back and one forward. On other days, Dale took three steps forward and zero back. Now Dale has confidently stepped into a firm belief in his new story. He embraces his worth. He's committed to conditioning his thoughts and actions to live his new, energizing story.

Step Four: To solidify his commitment, I encouraged Dale to trash his old story. He chose to tear out his old left-column story, wad it up, and toss it into his fire pit, where it disappeared forever. This action had a massive and lasting impact on Dale's ability to move forward.

Once Dale embraced his new story, he left his destructive relationship, embraced a social lifestyle void of smoking and hangovers, began working with a physical trainer, and was hired by his dream architectural firm! Dale shows up for the life he wants because he changed his life's narrative and chose an energizing story.

IT'S YOUR TURN

Now that you know the flow, it's time for you to rewrite your story. *Ready, set, go!*

Step One: Using a sheet of paper with two columns, write your story in the left column exactly as you hear it going through your mind. Write your name at the top of the page, designating it as your story.

Step Two: To energize the rewrite of your story, separate what's true and fabricated about yourself by circling only the factual points in your left-column list. The truths you circle are part of your new story. Some truths will be circumstances outside of your control. Ask yourself, *"If I were committed to finding an empowering meaning to attach to this truth, what would that be?"*

> *Positive language—what you write, say to yourself, or voice aloud—will train your mind to tell stories that serve you.*

Step Three: In the right column, write out your new, energizing story as you want it to be, beginning with the true points you circled in the left column, noting truths and new meanings.

Use the present tense and positive language. Avoid words like "don't" (substitute *I want, I am*), "but" (substitute *and*), and "I have to, I need to, I should" (substitute *I want to, I get to, I choose to*). Positive language—what you write, say to yourself, or voice aloud—will train your mind to tell stories that serve you. With conditioning, powerful storytelling will become natural for you.

Step Four: Cut the columned paper in half to separate the left side (old story) and right side (new story). Now you have visual representations of your exhausting old narrative and your energizing new one.

Here's the fun part: Destroy your exhausting story! Tear it up. Burn it. Boil it. Flush it. Do whatever is meaningful for you to send it to its final resting place. Make it powerful and memorable, mentally and physically. Say aloud with conviction, "I commit to let my old story go!"

To make the destruction of your old story even more impactful, tell a trusted friend what you did and send that individual a picture of how you destroyed it. Or invite that person to the demolition celebration!

Another impactful idea to add to this exercise is to put heavy things, such as books, cans, or rocks into a backpack. Wear the heavy backpack for a bit before you destroy your old story. Immediately after you trash it, put down the backpack. This exercise gears your nervous system to remember that your old story was a heavy burden. The new one is light and invigorating! Get creative in associating pain with the old account and pleasure with the new one in whatever clever way is meaningful for you.

It's okay if you don't believe your new story just yet. Be patient with yourself and realize it took time to form the old story, so it may take time to embrace your new one. Writing it down as you want it to be creates both a brain print and a heart print. With time and conditioning, you'll build trust in your new story.

You have the power to utilize what life brings you instead of being used by it.

Get creative with how to condition yourself with the new story. Declare it. Speak it aloud. Use body motions. Post it where you can see it every day. Recite its truths at least twice daily to meld them into your physiology and create new neural pathways in your brain.

You have the power to utilize what life brings you instead of being used by it. As the sole narrator of your story, own it! Tell a powerful story that emboldens and energizes you!

CHAPTER 5

SPEAK GOOD MAGIC

"Words are, in my not-so-humble opinion, our most
inexhaustible source of magic. Capable of both
inflicting injury, and remedying it."[8]

—DUMBLEDORE

Do you believe in magic? The truth is, you speak it every day. Albus Dumbledore, Headmaster of Hogwarts School, where Harry Potter discovered his magic and calling, got it right when he said, "Words are our most inexhaustible source of magic."[9]

So, how are you using your words? Are they inflicting injury or remedying it? Recognizing the difference and choosing to speak authentically and positively (to yourself and others) are magical ways to cast a life you love. No wand required!

As a life coach, I listen closely to syntax when my clients chat with me. *Do their words describe feelings or facts?* Word choice speaks volumes about what's going on in one's head—and heart.

Lately, I find myself clarifying syntax even more often since launching sentences

> *Word choice speaks volumes about what's going on in one's head—and heart.*

with "I feel like . . ." has become a cultural norm. However, living all in for the life you want is far more than a feeling. It requires the truth. And as old school as it may sound, "The truth will set you free!"[10]

Mastering a magic spell required Harry Potter to practice repeatedly to get the wording just right. Likewise, developing the craft of choosing the most accurate words to describe your situation at any given moment requires practice focused on truth, not just feelings: *Are you starving or just hungry? Are you struggling or just sad today? Did someone make you angry, or did you respond to what they said with anger? Do you have anxiety, or do you feel a bit anxious?* (The first is a clinical diagnosis; the latter is a valid feeling—a wave of emotion.)

Word choice matters. Recognizing why you choose specific words and phrases to describe a situation can tell you a lot about what may be shaping your interpretation of that event and your chosen wording.

Your feelings about something don't necessarily qualify as truth.

Here's a sobering fact: Your feelings about something don't necessarily qualify as truth. In any given situation, it's essential to recognize what part of an associated feeling is rooted in truth (if any of it). Truth is the gravity that will keep you balanced.

Digging down to the source of a feeling to uncover its truth is a fair and honest way to live. Reacting (to a feeling), without unearthing its source, plants you in shallow ground and can leave you mired in mud that can splatter on others. Feelings not grounded in truth are hazardous when relating to people because they can lead to reactive, false accusations.

Here's a life truth to guard carefully: *When you blame someone else for your feelings, you carry a weighty responsibility for more than yourself. Feelings-fueled words can cause injury.* Assess your emotions before you speak, and dig for the facts.

USE FEELINGS AS CLUES

Earlier in the book, you discovered the importance of knowing what you want—and that living all in for a life you love requires focusing on what you want. Intentional vocabulary is an integral part of that focus. Your language drives your focus, so choose your rhetoric wisely. Remember, you get what you focus on.

> *Choose words that keep you headed toward what you want, not what you don't.*

Words you speak aloud or to yourself move you in one direction or another. That's the momentum of good magic! Choose words that keep you headed toward what you want, not what you don't.

Here's a simple way to use your feelings as test strips for helpful vs. harmful vocabulary. I call it, The Four F's:

1. *Feel it.* Stop and get curious (instead of cuckoo) when you feel a way you don't want to feel.
2. *Find it.* Next, ask yourself: *What words just went through my mind or out of my mouth?* (Check out these three often-spoken, feelings-based statements: "She made me so mad." "This is too hard." "I'm so tired I could die.") Whew! Those are a lot of exhausting words!

3. *Fact-check it.* Now, ask yourself, *What's the truth behind my initial statement?* (Think about the last time you were angry. Did someone or something *make* you mad? No. Plain and simple, you chose to respond with anger. No one else has the power to make you feel a feeling unless you grant them that power.)

4. *Frame it.* Here's a productive way to reframe that feeling: *I feel angry. Good for me; I'm aware of my emotions. Is anger a necessary response to this situation? How do I want to feel instead of angry? I can't control other people. What can I control? What emotion do I have the power to choose right now? How will choosing that emotion make me feel?*

   Consider the following statement: *"This is too hard. I'm so tired, I could die."* What if something is hard to do and something else? Practice catching yourself and reframing your words. *"This is hard and character-building. I'm tired, and it was a good day."*

You can speak the truth *and* move forward by reframing or tweaking your words to your advantage. Here's a simple trick that works magic: Substitute the word *but* with the word *and* whenever you speak or write. Notice how the switch makes you feel. You can say, "I've had a disappointment, *but* I'm choosing to thrive," or "I've had a disappointment, *and* I'm choosing to thrive." The first presupposes disappointment is a threat to thriving. The second presupposes disappointment is a natural part of life.

> **Substitute the word but with the word and whenever you speak or write.**

Language matters. The wording, "I'm a great mom, *and* I get angry sometimes," is honest and empowering. "I'm a great mom, *but* I get angry sometimes," disempowers me because it assumes my strengths somehow rose to the surface despite another part of me.

Choose magical words. When you acknowledge others or yourself for something, let it be in addition to all that makes up the beauty of humanity, not despite an aspect of it. Refuse to relegate your life to "buts!" The tiny word *and* does big things! As you go through each day, play around with reframing your comments and notice how you feel. When you find words that inspire the feelings you want to have, condition yourself to use those words often.

> **Refuse to relegate your life to "buts!"**

Changing your vocabulary takes intentional repetition until your new word choices become second nature. This word-flip doesn't feel natural at first, and it doesn't happen overnight. Speaking good word magic involves intentionally choosing how to show up for a situation and deciding how to label it.

There's a fantastic bonus when you get into the rhythm of choosing magical words: You'll influence others around you to do the same. (How's that for paying something forward!)

Here's how to practice word magic any time you catch yourself talking aloud about challenging circumstances. Ask yourself:

Did it happen to me, or did it happen, and I was there?

Since word choice differentiates fact from feelings, did someone make me feel a certain way, or did I choose to respond to them emotionally?

_____

What growth opportunity did I gain from this circumstance?

_____

_____

Did this circumstance trigger an old feeling in me? If so, what?

_____

_____

When was the first time I felt this way? What happened to make me feel this way?

_____

Is that still happening? If not, out of habit, am I reacting as though it is?

_____

What is a better way to respond to my current situation than repeating old reactions?

These questions tap into your curiosity about the definitions you wrap around your circumstances. By answering them, you dig down to the source of a pattern, so you can expose it and change it to your advantage. (It's ok to momentarily peek into your past to find the trigger of a pattern if that knowledge enables you to propel toward the life you want. Remember that it's an old story, far from the one you want to live now.)

How you define a circumstance in words (internal or external) becomes your perception of that event. And your perception is your story. So, words lead to perception. Perception leads to your story. Your story leads to your focus. And you get what you focus on. Getting the life you want requires you to choose your words wisely.

In the movie *Harry Potter and the Chamber of Secrets*, Albus Dumbledore tells Harry, "It is not our abilities that show what we really are; it is our choices."[11] That's incredible wisdom!

Each day, choose empowering words that show what you are. The life you want to live will follow! Dump words that don't serve you, and choose words that do.

Bottom line? You control and are entirely responsible for your choices, beliefs, and emo-

Dump words that don't serve you, and choose words that do.

tions. You own the meanings you attach to your circumstances. You can choose to live as if all disappointments in life are happening to you, or you can become aware that circumstances occur, and with each one, you get to choose how you perceive that situation.

ABUNDANT MINDSET

Frodo and Gandalf, our favorite duo from *The Lord of the Rings*, had a heart-to-heart chat one day about things not going as planned, and it speaks well of the positive spirit and making more out of less:

> "*'I wish it need not have happened in my time,' said Frodo.*
>
> *'So do I,' said Gandalf, 'and so do all who live to see such times. But that is not for them to decide. All we have to decide is what to do with the time that is given us.'*"[12]

There's so much potential bounty in the time given us. Difficult life changes and being different build character. Reframe disappointments as what's gained instead of lost. Choose words and actions that do that. Then notice what happens inside your soul. Triumph rises!

An abundance mindset speaks of what's gained. A scarcity mindset speaks of what's lost. Give this a whirl: For a week, speak only about what's gained—and see what happens. *What if instead of losing weight, you gain lightness? Instead of quitting an addiction, you gain clarity (i.e., gain sobriety instead of quitting drinking)? What if you stop*

Reframe disappointments as what's gained instead of lost.

being a victim and start being a victor? What if you grieve by honoring the beauty that person or thing added to your life?

You get what you speak. It becomes your truth. Choose your words wisely.

One final quote from the wise Dumbledore says it all: *"Happiness can be found, even in the darkest of times, if only one remembers to turn on the light."*[13]

Flip the switch, my friend. It's magic.

CHAPTER 6

CULTIVATE YOUR
MIND GARDEN

"What happens inside your head will find
its way outside—into your life."[14]

—HENRY CLOUD

Think about your thoughts because they matter—a lot. Acclaimed English poet William Wordsworth once wrote, "Your mind is the garden, your thoughts are the seeds; the harvest can either be flowers or weeds.[15]

So, what thought seeds are you planting these days? Psychologist Dr. Henry Cloud, author of the best-selling books *Boundaries* and *The Secret Things of God*, tells us: "What happens inside your head will find its way outside—into your life."[16]

That means you must pay attention to your thoughts because they impact your actions. Want to know the secret for growing flowers instead of weeds in your mind? *Question your thoughts!*

Your life harvest is a thinking thing, and your mind is immensely fertile. When properly cultivated, your mind garden will grow

You wouldn't plant kudzu in a flower garden, so don't allow negative thoughts to take root in your mind.

the bountiful life you want to live. However, you can get tangled up in weeds when negative thoughts invade your mind. You wouldn't plant kudzu in a flower garden, so don't allow negative thoughts to take root in your mind.

Life coaches listen for harmful, lousy questions clients often ask themselves. These questions are often rhetorical. *What's wrong with me? Why am I here? Why am I such a loser? Why can't I be more like _____?*

Sound familiar? If so, it's time to pull those thought weeds because your brain doesn't know that negative questions are rhetorical. Your mind will answer them, and it's nearly impossible to find a positive answer to those questions.

If your mind, consciously or subconsciously, answers the question, *What's wrong with me?* with any form of *I'm not enough*, you risk believing that lie and creating a negative pattern in your brain—a weed that can grow deep, tangled roots. Whether you're aware of it or not, your brain will respond to a lousy question with a lousy answer. You'll tell yourself the story of how and why you aren't enough—and that story will seep into and poison every aspect of your life.

Becoming aware of your thoughts is the first step to interceding so you can begin asking productive questions and thinking constructive thoughts. How do you do this? By using your feelings as alarm bells. When you feel a way you don't want to feel:

- stop and notice what question went through your head;
- identify it as lousy;
- celebrate your awareness;
- reseed that lousy question with a productive one.

Here are some examples of reseeding your thoughts:

Lousy question: *What's wrong with me?*

Productive questions: *What's great about me? Why am I more than enough? How lovable am I? What does my higher power say about my worth? How am I the perfect person for the task at hand?*

Lousy question: *Why can't I be more like _____?*

Productive questions: *What makes me unique? What are my special gifts? What's exciting about not being like anyone else?*

Lousy question: *Why do I have to sit through this useless meeting?*

Productive questions: *What's something new I can appreciate about the individual in front of me? What's great about this moment? What's something productive I can use from this meeting?*

Notice your internal dialogue, be it a question or a thought. Trade what doesn't serve you for something better! Take small steps. Even if you don't believe your new answers, speak them aloud for now. The belief will follow. You'll grow into your newly conditioned narrative. With practice, you'll have what you want.

In *The Secret Things of God*, Henry Cloud tells us, "Whatever you put to use will grow." So, choose to use thoughts that will grow your mind and take you forward. Choose to

> **Notice your internal dialogue, be it a question or a thought. Trade what doesn't serve you for something better!**

yank thought weeds. Celebrate that you can ditch those lousy thoughts and reseed your mind to produce the life you want to live.

DIG FOR TRUTH

In William Young's groundbreaking book, *The Shack*, Mack feels a rush of intense anguish. He thinks, *"I feel so lost."* That's when the Truth Teller steps in: *"A hand reached out and squeezed his, and didn't let go. 'I know, Mack. But it's not true. I am with you, and I'm not lost. I'm sorry it feels that way, but hear me clearly. You are not lost.'"*[17]

> One of the most potent questions my training taught me to ask is the simplest: Is that true?

Truth is beautiful and bright, especially when negative feelings darken your mind without warning. One of the most potent questions my training taught me to ask is the simplest: Is that true?

Those three simple words, posed as a thought-provoking question, can transform your thinking and help you purge lies you may have been telling yourself for years, things like:

"I'll never be able to _____."
"The life I want doesn't happen to people like me."
"Because of a painful event from my past, it's impossible for me to _____."
"I don't have enough money to live the life I want."
"Because of my disability, I cannot _____."

If you hear any of these lies creep through your head, stop. Celebrate your awareness. Then ask, *Is that true?* Philippians 4:8a tells us, *". . . Fix your thoughts on what is true . . ."* The patterns you've established may fight to answer *yes* when a lie creeps through your mind like invasive kudzu. That's when you must dig, challenge that pattern, and ask, *Is it really true? Is it possible it isn't true?* And if still tempted to believe the lie, challenge it further by asking, *What if it weren't true? What if I choose to believe it isn't true? How would a substituted positive declaration sound?*

You don't have to believe a substituted positive declaration is true immediately. You'll make it your new pattern with time and conditioning. Eventually, it will become your new truth.

THOUGHTS ABOUT OTHERS

Sometimes, digging for truth involves thoughts about others. Let's say you're dreading a meeting with someone whom you feel is difficult. When the words "difficult person" flash through your mind, it's an excellent time to question that thought.

Is that true?

Is this person really difficult?

Is it possible that I have chosen to believe this person is difficult?

Do I have examples of incidents when this person wasn't difficult?

What are those examples?

It's a good idea to write down such examples because this helps shift how you think. (Remember, using actual pen and paper will help lock in these shifts best by getting them into your physiology.)

Let's say that, in one example you listed, the person (we'll call him Ted) was generous. Now ask yourself:

If I believe Ted is generous, how do I feel?

How will I feel during my interaction with Ted when I focus on the fact that he's generous?

How will I communicate with Ted if I believe he is generous and easy to interact with?

When you worry about another person's behavior, you give away your power to control your happiness.

Shifting the way you think takes a lot of pressure off your emotions. You can't control other people or all your circumstances; however, you can manage your interpretation of other people and your circumstances. You can control how you think about things and your response to others and events. And, the truth is, what's the harm in believing someone is also something beneficial in addition to or instead of difficult if it will lead to healthier emotions for you and a more productive meeting?

Cultivating a healthy mind garden is a thinking thing. When you worry about another person's behavior, you give away your power to control your happiness. Take back your power over what you can control—yourself, your beliefs, the questions you entertain, and your interpretation of your circumstances.

My client, Amber, an accomplished CPA, came to coaching when she began feeling intense stress at work. She said her supervisor's "abrasive, difficult, and controlling personality made her anxious."

Viktor Frankl, a psychiatrist and holocaust survivor, knew difficult people. In his book *Man's Search for Meaning,* Frankl teaches us, *"In the concentration camps, for example, in this living laboratory and on this testing ground, we watched and witnessed some of our comrades behave like swine while others behaved like saints. Man has both potentialities within himself; which one is actualized depends on decisions but not on conditions."*[18]

Amber and I cultivated an exercise plan to shift her mindset and decisions rather than her conditions with Frankl's wisdom in mind. Amber committed to stick to the exercise for one workweek, regardless of her natural pattern to push against it. Here's what Amber excitedly reported back to me the following week:

I went to work Monday feeling hopeful, and then I suddenly felt anxious when I saw Debbie, my supervisor. Before she even spoke, I noticed stress in my body. So, I remembered my stress was a signal. I allowed my alarm bell to remind me to ask myself, What thought just went through my head? I noticed a lousy question: why can't I have a different supervisor? And then another question: Why does Debbie have to be so abrasive and controlling? (Amber's lousy questions had become so habitual, her brain asked them merely at the sight of her supervisor before any words or action had taken place). *Then, I honored my commitment to my mind shift, and I celebrated my awareness!*

(At this point in her story, using my outside voice, I gave Amber a huge atta-girl, "Whoop! Whoop!")

Amber continued:

I then questioned my lousy question and asked, is it true that Debbie is "always" abrasive and controlling? I wanted to react with a vigorous yes. Instead, I thought, No, not always. *I remembered that she was also very generous with her time and attention to training me to be better in my career skill set. And that Debbie plans lunches for our team and gives us gifts and incentives. I then flipped my lousy question to, "What do I appreciate about my supervisor?" And then I realized I'm fortunate to work with Debbie.*

I stuck with these two main thoughts for the rest of the week. When my patterned reaction was to be anxious or stressed in Debbie's company, I used that feeling to remind me to shift my focus to her generosity. It wasn't an easy shift and didn't come naturally to me. However, I honored my week-long commitment, and I believe I've created a new pattern now! My anxious feelings are diminishing, and I think they will soon disappear. Debbie does have a strong personality, and with that comes a strong dose of generosity. I choose to focus on that because it just feels better.

Choosing to see others in good light may also be contagious. They may decide to shine that day!

Coach Chris had a dance party in her mind for Amber! And, when you think about your thoughts and cultivate your mind garden, a dance party is in your future.

Remember, you get to choose the light in which you see others. Bad lighting will dim your emotional wellness. The Stoic philosopher Epictetus said, *"You are hurt the moment you believe yourself to be."* Choosing to see others in good light may also be contagious. They may decide to shine that day!

Phillipians 4:8-9 (MSG) guides us toward cultivating a bountiful mind garden:, *"Summing it all up, friends, I'd say you'll do best by filling your minds and meditating on things true, noble, reputable, authentic, compelling, gracious—the best, not the worst; the beautiful, not the ugly; things to praise, not things to curse . . ."* Wow! That's a lot of good stuff!

Whenever you feel uncertain about anything, remember to ask yourself, *Is it true?* Practice this self-questioning until it becomes second nature and part of your physiology and natural pattern. Dig for truth whenever your thoughts take a negative turn. With time and attention, you'll grow a life you love—a life filled with flowers.

CHAPTER 7

CHOOSE YOUR FOCUS

"It matters not how strait the gate, How charged
with punishments the scroll, I am the master of my fate:
I am the captain of my soul."[19]

—WILLIAM ERNEST HENLEY

eak performance requires focus. Choose your focus—or other people and things will choose for you. Take athletic performance, for example. In golf, you focus on your swing and where you want the ball to land. Should your focus veer toward the last time you hit your ball on the fringe, you invite your brain to follow and repeat that undesired outcome. Thinking or saying aloud, *"Dang it! I always hit it in the sand on this hole,"* will, most likely, deliver a repeat performance.

My client, Gabe, a world-class collegiate swimmer, came to our weekly session with the desired outcome of getting his competition time back to where it had been the previous month. Gabe said he swam at his all-time slowest in his last two meets and couldn't figure out why.

I asked, "If you had to guess, why do you think you've performed slower?"

He thought and answered, "I'm not sure. Maybe I've lost my oomph for the sport. Or maybe I've peaked and will continue to get slower from here. Maybe my body is failing me."

Gabe was 20 years old.

I asked Gabe to close his eyes and take four deep breaths—inhale for four counts, exhale for four counts—then think back to the last swim meet that excited him—when he accomplished his personal best time or felt on top of the world after his performance.

"Ok. Got it," Gabe said.

"Great. With your eyes still closed, put yourself back in that moment. In the water, in your lane, on the final lap of your swim."

"Ok."

"Fantastic. Now tell me what you are focused on."

Gabe's answer was immediate. "My breath. Winning. How I just knew this was a personal best time."

"What else?" I asked.

"I'm focused on the wall. On the finish. On blowing past my competition. On speed. I'm focused on every cell in my body working with supernatural finesse and tirelessness."

"You're doing fantastic, Gabe. Keep your eyes closed and take a deep breath," I said. "Put yourself back in your most recent swim meet, the one from last week. You're in the water. Your competitors are in the lanes next to you. What were you focused on?"

Gabe breathed, thought, and answered, "I wasn't feeling good that day. It was a sucky day." (Gabe slipped out of his visualization of the moment and into the present.)

"Ok, Gabe. Take another breath and stay in that moment, as if last week's swim meet is happening now."

"Ok, I'm there."

"Super. Take another breath and sink even deeper into the moment—as if it's taking place now. Tell me what you're focused on."

"I'm focused on something my mom said before the meet. I'm worried I'm not good enough. I'm focused on my competitors winning. I'm thinking my time to shine is ending. I'm focused on the bottom of the pool. I'm sneaking peeks at the lanes next to me. I'm thinking how disappointed my mom will be in me."

"You're doing great, Gabe. What else?"

"I'm focused on how tired I am. I just want it to be over."

"Excellent work, Gabe. You can open your eyes."

"Wow!" he said. I had no idea. My focus was completely different in those two scenarios. I need to shift my focus back to when I was performing at my peak. If I change my focus, I'll change my time."

"Yes! So have you lost your oomph for swimming?"

"Not at all! I didn't even realize that I let my mom's comments get in my head."

"Do you want to talk about your mom's comments?" I asked.

"No, because they don't hold weight anymore."

"Still, you thought about them while swimming, so they had power over you."

Gabe responded, "Yeah. What she said isn't true, though. She meant no harm. I just let it trigger me back to my high school self. That guy lacked confidence."

"Going forward, how will you know if you've given someone, something, or some comment power over your focus?" I asked Gabe.

> "Going forward, how will you know if you've given someone, something, or some comment power over your focus?"

"I'll keep in tune with my feelings. If I feel sucky, I'll get curious about where my focus and thoughts are."

(Woohoo! Gabe was paying attention in previous sessions.)

"And what will you do if that high school guy rears his low-confidence again?"

"I'll tell him to jump off the deep end. Ha!"

To reinforce Gabe's excellent work and lock in a future tool for him I asked, "If you gave that guy a name, what would it be?"

"Sucky Sam"

"And who's the guy who loves swimming and performs at his peak ability?"

"Gabe the Goat!"

"And what will Gabe the Goat tell Sucky Sam should he show up in the future?"

"You can sit this one out, Sucky. I'll take it from here!"

"Bravo, Gabe!"

Calling out and naming desired and undesired parts of yourself is an effective way to live all in. You'll want to ask some parts of you to take a back seat or exit the vehicle to live the life you want.

Gabe's desired outcome for that session was to get his time back to where it had been the previous month. He accomplished that and even achieved a new personal best. The outcome had everything to do with his focus during the competition.

Gabe learned that he had allowed a comment to trigger a lack of confidence he hadn't felt since high school. It was a subtle trigger, so Gabe wasn't aware he had let go of his focused edge. He didn't realize his emotions correlated to what his mom had said until he was in the visualization exercise. Once aware of this, Gabe knew his mom's comments were harmless. Gabe now knows to focus on what he wants for himself, or he'll risk allowing another person or event to determine his focus for him.

Choosing and controlling your focus seems simple, yet you'll want to stay vigilant about where your mind is wandering. To do this, remember your alarm bells. As you are about to deliver peak performance in any area of your life, pay attention to your feelings. Do

As you are about to deliver peak performance in any area of your life, pay attention to your feelings.

you notice hesitancy, stage fright, procrastination, timidity, or fear? That's your alarm bell! Celebrate the awareness. Those feelings aren't wrong; you'll want to use them as fuel instead of stumbling blocks. As soon as your alarm bell goes off, focus on the result you want and only the result you want. Visualize sticking the landing, sinking the putt, or finishing the task.

Here's a simple, focus-minded exercise: On a colorful piece of paper, write down what you want to focus on (or find a picture that illustrates it) and use it as a focal point throughout your day. (Consider making it your smartphone wallpaper.)

Go to your new focal point whenever an off-the-positive-track thought tries to hijack your focus—practice bouncing your mindset from what you don't want to what you do want. Soon your new focus will become your natural mind language. You'll train your brain to focus on where you want to go.

You get what you focus on, so focus on what you want, *not* what you don't want. Focus on what you can control, not on what you can't. Focus on what you have, not what's missing. Mind your mind space. If a thought is junk, toss it out to make room for the good stuff.

If a thought is junk, toss it out to make room for the good stuff.

TAKE ACTION

Driving a car where you want to go involves focusing on the painted white lines ahead of you. You've had so much practice driving that you've conditioned yourself to stay between the white lines. Whether you're aware of it or not, you've mastered the art of driving deep into your muscle memory. You're mentally, physically, and emotionally a peak performer at driving.

With repetition, you'll master any skill with intentional focus (on the result you want) *plus* conditioning. Manifesting what you want involves visualization of the desired goal *plus* effort. James 2:17 (NIV) tells us, *"In the same way, faith by itself, if it is not accompanied by action, is dead."*

During an introduction call, I had a potential client (PC) tell me that he came to coaching to achieve his one-year goal of increasing his annual earnings by one million dollars. Here's how the conversation went:

Me: Great! Are there any hindrances to you achieving that outcome?

PC: Absolutely not!

Me: Super! So what do you need to do to achieve this result?

PC: I need to manifest it.

Me: Fantastic! We will work through several exercises and assignments to get you and keep you laser-focused on what you want.

PC: Awesome!

Me: What else do you want from our coaching relationship?

PC: That's it—for you to hold me accountable for manifesting the money. And teach me better ways to manifest if I'm doing it wrong.

Me: And do you also commit to putting in the work we come up with as the best strategies for accomplishing your outcome of earning one million more dollars in a year?

PC: Oh, I'm not interested in strategy. I believe in the Law of Attraction. You just need to make sure I don't get distracted from manifesting the money.

Me: I'm curious. How much are you earning annually now?

PC: 215K.

Me: And what are you doing to earn that money?

PC: I work in sales for a software company.

Me: To be certain I understand clearly—you earn 215K annually, and you want to up that this coming year by one million dollars that is solely manifested, not earned. Is that right?

PC: Yes. But manifesting the money is a means of earning it. I want to work for it by attracting it.

Me: I believe you can increase your earnings by one million dollars since that's what you want. I would love to help you get creative in doing that and hold you accountable for the methods we come up with together to achieve that outcome. For me to coach you, you'll need to commit to cooperating with me on your action plan. We'll also focus on your outcome, and I'll hold you accountable for attracting your goal. However, I cannot work with you if there's no follow-through action taken as part of getting what you want.

PC: I'm not interested in strategy. I've read many stories about people getting what they want on mental attraction alone.

Me: I believe in you. I don't believe I'm the right coach for you, though. I firmly believe that reaching goals requires focus *and* action, so I wish you the best in achieving the outcomes and life you want.

> **Getting the life you want requires showing up for it.**

If showing up for the life you want was a walk on easy street, this book wouldn't exist. And we wouldn't need mentors, teachers, or coaches. If you believe you can get the healing, relationship, career, wealth, or any desired outcome by attracting what you want with thoughts alone, what will happen to your belief system when what you want doesn't manifest itself? If you want all green lights on the way to work and believe you can attract that outcome with your thoughts, what happens when you encounter a red light? Life happens, and eventually, the light will be red.

Getting the life you want requires showing up for it. Showing up involves being all in physically, mentally, spiritually, and emotionally. Gabe attracted the swimming competition results he wanted because he showed up for practice. Over and over again!

On top of showing up physically, Gabe disciplined his mind to attract his desired results. He stayed alert to his emotions, focus, and physical training.

Gabe wouldn't have achieved what he desired by just thinking about it. He wouldn't have achieved his desired time by dipping one toe into the pool. Gabe showed up with all of himself. He was all in. Showing up with all of yourself for the life you want isn't easy. It takes focus—and action. So, mind your thoughts and get moving, my friend, because you can't just think your best; you must take action to make it happen.

CHECK YOUR LENS

Right now is the ideal time to check the lens through which you view all circumstances. You can choose to focus on what energizes you or what doesn't. To achieve the results you desire physically, mentally, emotionally, and spiritually, you must focus on what you want. Choosing well stops fear and panic from spreading. Choosing well multiplies and spreads love, joy, peace, patience, kindness, faithfulness, gentleness, and self-control.

Our daughter, Chloé, had the privilege of studying in Italy for a semester during college. My husband, Scott, and I visited her there. We got to walk through the Basilica di Santa Maria del Fiore and the Duomo Cathedral in Florence—and climb the 15th-century old spiral staircase (463 steps to the top).

Scott and I love adventure and usually *just go* without a ton of research. We began our staircase ascent, eager and energized to *climb the stairs quickly and get to the view.* The higher we climbed, the narrower the walls and ceiling became. Scott, 6'2," began slouching farther down with each step up.

At what I guessed was the halfway point, Scott stopped. He didn't say a word, yet I assumed he couldn't fit his body into the stairwell if we moved forward. So I stopped.

Scott was likely pausing to take the adventure all in, yet I focused on a false appearance that climbing higher was physically impossible. I chose to see the walls, ceiling, and staircase *closing in on us.* I saw several other visitors in the spiral staircase below me. There was no room to turn back and descend past them. I considered letting panic and claustrophobia overwhelm me. And then I didn't.

There was nowhere to go but up, so there was nowhere to shift my focus but up. I traded my assumption of what we couldn't do for a vision of what we could. Thousands of people before me had done the same climb and had pictures to prove it. A brochure picture of the spectacular view from the top of the staircase flooded my mind. I focused on that, and we continued upward.

Choose peace over panic; you're only a few steps from living the life you want.

We were not halfway to the top; we were twenty steps away! We had climbed 443 steps, and I almost quit with twenty to go because of my blurry focus. We emerged out of the stairwell tunnel to a breathtaking view of Florence. And I have pictures to prove it!

You are not a quitter. You push through tight, dark passageways until you see the light because you focus on the view from the top.

Keep it up! You are so close. Choosing your focus will refine your grit even more. Choose peace over panic; you're only a few steps from living the life you want.

CHAPTER 8

CREATE POSITIVE PATTERNS

"We are what we repeatedly do.
Excellence, then, is not an act, but a habit."[20]

—WILL DURANT (INTERPRETING ARISTOTLE)

When you're obsessed with something, it monopolizes your focus. That focus can drive you toward where you want to go in life—or pitch you into a muddy ditch. The great news is that you know who you are and what you want in life, and you can ignite your resourcefulness to create positive thought and behavior patterns worthy of beautiful obsession.

The first step toward creating patterns that serve you is to shed the shame of past choices. Shame is a wet blanket that can douse your resourcefulness. Shed it. Think of your past decisions, habits, distractions, and obsessions as stepping stones that paved the way to where you are now—ready to live life all in. If you pay attention and remain teachable, the path forward is clear. You've set your mind on the life you want, and your higher power will guide you to the best way to get there.

Shame is a wet blanket that can douse your resourcefulness. Shed it.

CHOICES ROOTED IN GROWTH

To illustrate the beauty of creating positive patterns, I'll be transparent. During my teens, twenties, and early thirties, I used alcohol, initially to connect and socialize, and later to numb emotional discomfort in my life. And it worked—until it didn't.

I recognized that alcohol was an unhealthy distraction, so I abstained for fourteen years. Then, for six months, I chose to add it back into my life. I thought mature me could enjoy social drinking since I had eliminated the situations I falsely believed alcohol had once numbed for me.

Here's my truth: I changed; however, for me, alcohol and its complexity had not. Although alcohol didn't dominate my life during those six months, it certainly diminished it and impeded my love for living all in.

During my six months of social drinking, I greatly missed my abstinence. I longed for it. I yearned for my energy and the distraction-free lifestyle that I knew so well. I missed my authentic self and how alcohol-free me accepted my God's grace, no strings attached. I missed those things far more than social drinking. I happily discovered that alcohol-free is the best way to be me.

My awareness prompted me to shift my focus to a beautiful obsession with abstinence. I chose to create a positive pattern that gave me the freedom to be my favorite self. My refreshed perspective reinforced who I am and what I want.

These days, I view living alcohol-free as a reflection of how my God created me—highly sensitive to people, places, and things. I celebrate that my body and spirit don't blend well with alcohol, and I use 1 Peter 5:8 (NIV) as my guardian of sorts: *"Be alert and of sober mind. Your enemy the devil prowls around like a roaring lion looking for someone to devour."*

Some people can remain alert and sober while enjoying an alcoholic beverage. To them, I smile and say, "Cheers!" as I drink my mocktail. The positive pattern I've chosen works for me. I don't feel deprived when I abstain. Instead, because of my choice to focus on a beautiful obsession with abstinence, I'm free to be the real me!

I want you to know the freedom of focusing on beautiful obsessions that bring out the real you. To pivot toward that positive mindset, first acknowledge that you'll feel deprived if you believe you're missing out on something. That lack, known as a scarcity mindset, can lead to a romanticization of whatever you perceive you're going to miss. A scarcity mindset risks substituting one unhelpful pattern with a different one to numb the discomfort of deprivation (For example: You stop smoking, and you start inhaling sugary snack foods).

Old habits and obsessions have no power over you when you refuse to relinquish control to them.

A living-all-in mindset embraces a truthful examination of the patterns you want and don't want for what they genuinely are and where they lead you. To step toward that, first give yourself some much-needed grace to focus on facts. One of the exciting things about creating positive patterns is that you get to live shame-free. Old habits and obsessions have no power over you when you refuse to relinquish control to them. *What a relief!*

And here's more great news. You don't have to create positive patterns on your own. You can allow others to help you achieve them. Start with your creator, who empowers you from within to create the positive patterns you want for your life. Your creator is in the business of growing you, not crushing you. (If you had a difficult parent, you might have trouble believing this; however, your higher power is always on your side. *Always*.) And through vulnerability within a like-minded community, support makes creating positive patterns sustainable. Asking for help is inner strength in action!

Many people I've coached say they used substances because they didn't want to feel certain emotions as keenly. However, numbing pain also numbs growth toward abundant joy and freedom.

When you show up for life, even the painful parts, you get to experience a creator who carries you when you cannot take another step. When you ask for help, you experience a supernatural power—and a divine acceptance your human mind cannot fully comprehend. You get to experience living grace.

Here's an exercise to help you embrace the real you.

Ask yourself:

What discomfort am I choosing to numb?

_____

_____

How has numbing this served me?

_____

_____

What has numbing my discomfort cost me?

_____

_____

What has it cost those I love?

_____

_____

What will it cost my future if I continue to numb this?

_____

_____

What is the cost of choosing to feel life instead of numbing?

_____

_____

Is this greater or less than the cost of continuing to numb?

_____

_____

What will I gain when I lay down my numbing patterns to be able to show up for my life?

_____

_____

How will this benefit my loved ones?

_____

_____

What would my life be like if I changed this now?

_____

_____

How does this make me feel?

_____

_____

Now, ask yourself one more question:

Because the obsession I want to leave behind drains me of strength and joy, what lifestyle choices bring me the most strength and joy?

_____

_____

_____

By answering those questions, you can get to the heart of what has been distracting you and focus on what you want. Then you get to decide how to show up for your life—and the people you want to surround yourself with to help you live it.

EXERCISE YOUR STRENGTHS

My client, Angela, was riddled with guilt because she ate lots of carbohydrates and didn't understand why she couldn't stop. When we unpacked this pattern, we discovered Angela had comforted herself with bagels and other carbs when her sister passed. Angela never associated her eating pattern with that event until our coaching sessions.

Once Angela realized she used bagels to soothe herself and cope through a painful season, she discovered she was tapping into a strength. She could have taken pills, drank too much, or lashed out at others. Instead, she ate bagels.

Angela discovered that there's no right or wrong way to grieve.

For her, carbs were her way of surviving a season. This awareness freed her to decide she didn't need to carbo-load going forward. She saw her past behavior as a strength, which empowered her to make the wise, lower-carb food choices that now serve her well.

So, ask yourself:

Is it possible that I entertained an obsession or the habit I now want to get rid of, not out of weakness but out of strength? _____

Did I use that habit to survive? To cope? _____

Did it serve me in some way for a while? If so, how?

_____

_____

Is it serving me now? _____

Will it serve me moving forward? _____

What other strengths do I have that would serve me better?

_____

_____

What are some healthy obsessions and coping habits I could pick up?

_____

_____

I once heard Oprah Winfrey share advice Maya Angelou gave her regarding regrets: *"You did in your twenties what you knew how to do. And when you knew better, you did better."*[21]

There's deep-soul wisdom in those words! So, now that you know how to replace your old ways with new, positive ones, here's a simple way to stay committed.

On an index card, write *COST* at the top of one side and *GAIN* at the top of the other. Using your answers to the previous questions, list the costs of continuing an unwanted pattern. Flip the card over, and list what you'll gain by changing your undesirable pattern to a positive.

Keep the card with you. Take out the card when tempted to do what you don't want to do. Remind yourself of the costs and benefits associated with your actions. Repeatedly associating benefits with what you want and consequences to what you don't will condition your brain to move toward what your heart desires.

You get to decide which behaviors you associate with gains and costs. You get to train your brain to create positive patterns. This process burns off negative patterns that

> *Repeatedly associating benefits with what you want and consequences to what you don't will condition your brain to move toward what your heart desires.*

are keeping you off balance, things you're obsessing over without realizing it, and stuff distracting you from becoming the best you.

Now that you know better, you can do better—one positive pattern at a time.

CHAPTER 9

PRACTICE GRACE

"Grace is the face that love wears
when it meets imperfection."[22]

—JOSEPH R. COOKE

Your all-in-life won't be perfect. There will be sweat-filled days that yield little or nothing. Kick-in-the-teeth disappointments will grimace your grin. And, most likely, a few *What in the world was I thinking?* scenarios will leave you scratching your head. (We've all been there, right?)

With the blister of imperfection in mind, make sure you give yourself and others grace—and lots of it. Grace, you see, is good for the soul. It's like a healing balm that soothes a bad sunburn. You'll want to slather plenty of it on yourself and those around you because life can sting a bit, sometimes a lot.

Grace is a short word with a long reach. It's a spontaneous gift that's generous, totally unexpected, and undeserved. It's given freely to anyone who chooses to accept it, no strings attached. (Yourself included.)

Grace has a stunningly high "Wow!" factor. And a little bit of it can make a huge difference. That's one reason I begin each day with this prayer: *God, help me practice grace and forgiveness for myself and others rather than judgment, blame, and rules.*

I confess the concept of grace didn't make sense to me in my younger years. I lived under the illusion that I was in control of my worth. I strived for perfection under a false belief it was an attainable standard. *What did grace have to do with it?* Well, it turns out, a whole heck of a lot.

> We cannot accept grace when we believe we're in control of our worth.

Here's the reality check for imperfect humans: We cannot accept grace when we believe we're in control of our worth. And when we're unable to receive grace, we cannot offer it to others. The flow of grace is as liquid as that.

Here's where stuff gets a bit more complicated: *Self-esteem can plummet under the drench of stress and the weight of exhaustion. Pride and judgy behavior follow.* Sounds backward, right? It isn't. You see, pride doesn't only flaunt itself through conceit and pompousness; it also masquerades as low self-worth.

I call this masquerade "reverse pride." If you're isolated, stuck in your head, and miserable, your reverse pride won't accept your creator's grace; it will shun your higher power's positive words about you.

Reverse pride is controlling and demands that the things you say and think about yourself are the truth. This form of pride is dangerous because it seeks to supplant your higher power. It adamantly attests *I know best what I'm worth and what I deserve.* Reverse pride sets nearly impossible standards for excellence and then launches "You're a failure!" bombs directly at you know who.

And the missiles don't stop there. When you cannot apply any more pressure on yourself to perform, reverse pride targets others as judgment and blame when things don't go as you expect.

Not to accept grace is to say *I know best what I don't deserve*. Not to extend grace to others says *I know what's best for them*. That's a stifling way to live!

Showing up for the life you want with a face of grace is all about love. Loving others flows from loving yourself. And that kind of love relies on humility. My pastor, Doug Miller, put it this way: "Proud people don't love well, but forgiven people do."[23]

LET GRACE IN

Grace is the key to freedom. A whole new world opens up when you freely accept and give grace. Here are some questions to help you embrace it.

What accolades or criticisms do I insist on controlling in my life?

_____

_____

Is there an area of my life I'm not happy with or want to change?

_____

_____

What is my belief about myself in that area?

_____

_____

What would I notice if I became willing to set aside that belief to hear what my higher power says about me?

_____

_____

Am I willing to believe what my higher power says about me?

_____

_____

If not yet, am I willing to act as if I believe what my higher power claims is true about me, just for now?

_____

_____

You just let grace in by having the courage and tenacity to answer those questions. So, keep going!

Whatever your spiritual faith, surrendering to a divine power greater than yourself opens you to an even more abundant life. You get to absorb and shine the light of grace—and you're off the hook of perfectionism!

Ask yourself:

In my own faith, how does the truth about surrendering to an even more abundant life feel to me?

_____

_____

My higher power created me and knows best what fills me up. What are those things?

_____

_____

Is there an area of my life that frustrates me?

_____

_____

Have I been relying on myself to control this area?

_____

_____

Now, give up your illusion of control in that area for just one moment. Close your eyes, take a breath, and imagine your higher power stepping into this moment. Take another breath, then exhale even more control. Breathe out every last bit of your influence. Allow only your creator to lead at this moment. Ask yourself:

What do I notice?

_____

_____

What is different?

_____

_____

What goodness do I notice my creator proclaiming over me?

_____

_____

What favor is bestowed on this situation or area of my life?

What did grace heal in my life?

Anchor your answers in your soul. Use whatever meaningful tool you choose to continually remind yourself who you are when you embrace grace. Grab a physical token to carry as a reminder— or create a movement like snapping your fingers or clapping your hands.

For me, saying, "Let go and let God!" works. Letting go doesn't mean giving up or choosing to do nothing. It takes a monumental amount of energy and effort to set aside my ego and let my God be God. I work hard at embracing grace because surrender doesn't come naturally to me. However, my God has taught me that the act of surrendering is a standing position.

The act of surrendering is a standing position.

I bask in the wisdom of 2 Corinthians 1:9 and 12:9 to help me stand in the warmth of grace and rely on my God for strength. In that bright warmth, I've discovered that surrender nurtures true freedom.

"In fact, we expected to die. But as a result, we stopped
relying on ourselves and learned to rely only on God,
who raises the dead."

2 CORINTHIANS 1:9

". . . 'My grace is all you need.

My power works best in weakness.' So now I am glad
to boast about my weaknesses, so that the power
of Christ can work through me."

2 CORINTHIANS 12:9

Grace is a thing of beauty that grows even more stunning when
you embrace it for yourself and others. Believe in grace. Accept it.
Give it. Live in its warmth. It is the face of love.

CHAPTER 10

MOVE PAST YOUR PAST

"Courage isn't the absence of fear. It's doing what
you are afraid to do. It's having the power to let go of
the familiar and forge ahead into new territory."[24]

—JOHN C. MAXWELL

love being happy. So I choose to be responsible for my happiness. I choose to be grateful for my journey instead of being labeled by it. I opt to focus on what is, not what's missing. Embracing happiness is way more fun than marinating in unhappy memories.

What emotion do you love feeling? It doesn't have to be happy. Know what emotion you love, though. Do you love feeling at peace? Content? Brave? Confident? Choosing the emotional state you want for any given moment of your life is your right. You're the only person who gets to decide that. And if you're going to live all in, you'll want to choose emotions that move you forward and ensure you're showing up for the

Choosing the emotional state you want for any given moment of your life is your right.

life you want—instead of staying stuck in unhelpful emotional patterns.

For years, I didn't choose happiness. Instead, I believed that grinding over what I didn't love in my life would change it. I studied psychology in college and grad school because I wanted to help others (and also in an attempt to heal myself by analyzing my past behaviors). Grinding all those things out was an honest attempt at moving forward. I proceeded the best I knew how for the season I was living at the time. However, focusing on what I wanted to leave behind only kept me stuck in it.

Remember the wisdom of Maya Angelou? "When you know better, do better." When I finally knew better, I shifted my focus to what I wanted, thankful that my past was the perfect environment to teach me what was necessary to become the woman I am today. These days, I focus on what I'm grateful for in my present and the results I want in my future.

Remember when you decided what you wanted? Are you focusing on things that move you forward? If so, *Happy Dance time!* However, if your focus these days is more often looking back at what you want to move past, it's time to get unstuck.

Don't get me wrong; focusing on your history is helpful—for a particular reason or season. It becomes unhelpful when you camp there. When you build your emotional home from feelings related to days gone by, you're stuck with residual pain as your primary identity.

Moving forward doesn't mean ignoring your past or pretending trauma didn't happen. It requires facing it and having the courage to ask for help from a therapist, counselor, mentor, coach, or friend. Once you do that, celebrate your awareness and intention. You get to decide what you take from your past and what you don't. There's no right or wrong way to heal. And in determining the way that works best for you, continually ask yourself, Is what I'm taking with me from this past situation moving me forward, keeping me stuck, or moving me backward?

Is what I'm taking with me from this past situation moving me forward, keeping me stuck, or moving me backward?

An acquaintance of mine, Lanie, was going on a mission trip overseas. The trip leader was clear: *"You have to carry your luggage, so pack light."*

A few days before the trip, Lanie sat in a crumpled heap in her bedroom, staring at three suitcases packed to the max. Recognizing that hauling all that stuff around the world solo would be dang near impossible, she called her well-traveled friend, Becca, for help.

After eyeing the three bulging suitcases, Becca hugged Lanie and then said, "Girlfriend, you are a fabulous person, and you have amazing places to go and wonderful things to do. All this baggage is going to weigh you down! You have to leave a bunch of this stuff behind to get to where you want to go. Trust me; I've been there! Let me help you lighten things up!"

Together, the two friends opened every suitcase and worked through the items needed for the trip and those that were just stuff Lanie always hauled around wherever she went. After no small amount of teeth grinding, the pile of ditched items grew larger and larger. Through tears, laughter, and a few cuss words, three suitcases shrank down to a small backpack and a wheeled duffle bag that included only Lanie's necessities (and a few things that gave her joy).

Lanie showed up for that transatlantic flight with nothing

weighing her down. She had a smile on her face and pep in her step because she knew what she wanted and had everything she needed for the trip of a lifetime.

CHANGE YOUR SHIRT

If you're still reading this book, you've chosen to show up for the life you want. Showing up requires taking what's helpful and dumping the rest. That's what showing up is about. It's choosing to move through the good, bad, and ugly instead of away from it.

Showing up isn't easy. There's no "just get over it" quick remedy for moving past the past. Likely there will be some tears, teeth grinding, and a few cuss words—maybe a lot of them as you unpack your baggage. (Dang it, life has sucky moments, doesn't it?)

In the next chapter, we'll dive deeper into how to ride the waves of pain; however, right now, close your eyes and ask yourself, *Am I identifying with my past or making it my identity?* There's a difference.

Am I identifying with my past or making it my identity?

Think of it this way: Wearing an old, comfortable t-shirt is easy. It feels good and energizes you. You often wear it when you go out with friends. It's a sure thing and a safe choice.

On the flip side, wearing that same t-shirt day after day is gross. It stinks and has lost fit, power statement, and good looks. Even your closest friends are tired of seeing you in it. They wonder why your choice is unrepresentative of your beautiful soul. That t-shirt, once a comfort, has become a curse—a smelly, tattered identity.

So, ditch that smelly shirt and choose a new one! Stepping

out of a familiar identity because it's no longer helpful and into the one you want takes courage. And you are brave, my friend. Acknowledge past pains, thank them for making you the incredible person you are today, then focus on the life you want. Here are some questions to help you move in that direction:

Acknowledge past pains, thank them for making you the incredible person you are today, then focus on the life you want.

When I meet someone for the first time, how do I represent myself?

_____

_____

_____

_____

What does the other person know about me after the first fifteen minutes of conversation?

_____

_____

_____

What are the parts of my identity that I love the most?

_____

_____

_____

_____

Do I step into and enjoy these parts of my identity? If not, why not?

_____

_____

Do I share the good stuff with others? If not, why not?

_____

_____

Have I limited my identity to a painful past story because it sets me apart, makes me feel special, or brings me comfort?

_____

_____

If so, how has narrowly representing myself prevented others from seeing the authentic me?

_____

_____

What has living as or longing for a past version of myself cost me?

_____

_____

Who am I now because of my past?

_____

_____

What is my story today?

_____

_____

_____

_____

What do I want my story to be moving forward?

_____

_____

_____

_____

_____

> **Don't allow your past to define you. Use it to refine and fuel you for the life you want.**

You get to decide how you represent yourself to yourself and others. Though you don't get to pick and choose all your life's circumstances, you determine those that define you.

Here's the truth: *Not every cloud has a silver lining; some clouds suck.* However, you don't have to stand under that gloom forever. You can choose to step into the sunshine that your storm cloud cleared for you.

You have the power, the presence, the guts, and the sheer determination to move forward. Don't allow your past to define you. Use it to refine and fuel you for the life you want.

This quote from author Paulo Coelho speaks to my soul, and I hope yours:

"You can either be a victim of the world or
an adventurer in search of treasure.

It all depends on how you view your life."[25]

Please, search for your treasure, my friend. Because you are one,
and your higher power has gifted you to the world.

CHAPTER 11

RIDE YOUR WAVE

"Suffering in and of itself is meaningless;
we give our suffering meaning by the way
in which we respond to it."[26]

—HAROLD KUSHNER

You can't avoid pain. Sooner or later, it will hit—hard. And although you can't avoid it, you can control how you respond to it.

Think of pain as a booming, violent wave that suddenly rises as you swim off the beach. You cannot escape its path; however, you do have a choice: You can ride that wave or let it pummel you.

If you choose to ride your wave, it's still going to hurt—a lot. You'll feel as if the intense power of pain and grief will crush you. And then, it doesn't. Instead, it carries and pushes you toward calmer water and shore.

Your other option is to get pulled under by the force of the wave and let it slam you to the ocean floor or onto rocks, crushing your spirit and trapping you in murky water where weird things grow. This stagnant pool becomes your new habitat, separating you from waves that can float you to the calm of the shore.

Pain happens. You grieve and lament. Natural pain in life is beautifully human. Choosing to remain miserable is not.

A fellow life coach, Mark, experienced his 13-year-old son Benjamin's passing because of a rare disease. I asked Mark how he made it to shore instead of getting stuck on the rocks of grief. Mark shared that he took the time he needed to fully grieve, lament, and embrace all his painful emotions. (This takes bravery and varying amounts of time for people.)

Natural pain in life is beautifully human. Choosing to remain miserable is not.

At first, Mark felt crushed and could not see an end to his mourning. Yet regardless of how he felt emotionally, Mark trusted that he wouldn't feel permanently crushed. (Forever changed, yes. Forever crushed, no).

Mark chose to ride his wave. He paid close attention to the narrative that he weaved around Benjamin's passing. Mark's coaching experience had taught him the importance of story. Using an exercise much like the one from Chapter 4, *Write Your Story*, Mark penned a narrative around the event that helped him lean into his reality, a story based on trust and belief.

Mark's initial story about Benjamin's physical death was *The worst thing that could have happened to me has happened.* With intention and effort, Mark conditioned himself to believe a different story, which he still trusts: *The worst thing that could have happened to me did not happen because the worst thing that could have happened to me would be if Benjamin were never born.*

Because Mark is a phenomenal life coach and understands the value of owning a powerful story, he's not only surviving his physical separation from Benjamin; he's thriving in his work. Mark is a gift to hundreds of others stuck in tide pools of pain. He helps people grieve beautifully and move toward shore, thus honoring the ones they miss—and honoring Benjamin.

HONOR YOUR SADNESS

Riding your wave of pain and grief involves giving honor to your sadness. In his book, *The Obstacle is the Way*, Ryan Holiday gives us insight: *"In its own way, the most harmful dragon we chase is the one that makes us think we can change things that are simply not ours to change."*[27]

When you acknowledge what there is to appreciate about life the way it is, you honor your sadness and embrace peace instead of expecting life to be the way it isn't. Not pain-free peace. But peace. This *heartset* keeps you from stagnating in a tide pool of sorrow. As an emotional being, you get sad and angry. You grieve. How you move through these emotions can either sabotage or heal you.

> *Riding your wave of pain and grief involves giving honor to your sadness.*

Grief doesn't follow a set of rules. And since it isn't linear, its hammer can slam down unexpectedly anytime. It looks different to each individual and takes varying time until the hammer slams less frequently and with less force.

There's no wrong or right way to move through painful emotions, only helpful and not helpful ways for yourself and others. Your unique experiences aren't in a textbook—and how you move through pain and ride the wave of it will be unique to you.

Since the fluidity of deep sadness often rises and pounces without warning, scheduling a time to be all in on your sorrow is a helpful way to honor your sadness and move forward through a painful season. This approach may sound simple, silly even, yet it's possible to be present for yourself, others, and life *while* you mourn, lament, and feel pain.

This approach to grieving can involve scheduling times (each day, hour, week—whatever works best for you) to engage certain feelings without being crushed. Author and speaker Yung Pueblo understands the cleansing power of engaging pain: *"It wasn't time that healed you, it was your courage to feel everything you used to run away from. Being with yourself and meeting your tension is hard, but it's the only way to release everything that's been bottled up inside of you. Your pain was simply asking for your attention."*[28]

> When you numb the pain, you numb everything else. So, you numb the good stuff too.

Honor your sadness by giving it the attention it needs to do its healing work. Scheduling a time into your day to feel pain won't remove it; grief is not a disease to be cured. However, healing is nurtured when you tenderly sit with your sadness.

Granted, hiding or running from your painful feelings can feel more comfortable than sitting with them. Here's the deal, though—when you numb the pain, you numb everything else. So, you numb the good stuff too. And eventually, a life without good feelings becomes uncomfortable.

Likewise, there are costs for facing your range of emotions. You'll risk hurt, vulnerability, time, and asking others for support. However, those exposures are far less perilous than the long-term risks linked with numbing your feelings, putting up a brave front, and staying busy to avoid processing your emotions.

Lamenting is necessary and natural. Staying stuck in despair permanently is not. Pain done well is beautiful because it's part of being human. There is, however, a difference between *natural pain* and *emotional misery*. Natural pain produces grit when you allow it to run its course and do its good work. Emotional misery produces negative results. It consumes time and energy and keeps you stuck.

The good news is that choosing to deal with emotional misery is within your control. Every hour of every day, it's your choice to live from a beneficial mindset or a miserable mindset. You can face pain from a beautiful human perspective without choosing to agonize emotionally.

How? For starters, use what you're learning in this book. Choose your focus, own your perspective, and weave a helpful story around your circumstances. In addition, maintain a physical self-care routine that serves you well. Mind your food, drink, and sleep intake and move your body. A painful season is rough enough without the distraction of feeling run down.

REACH OUT

I want to tenderly and firmly stress this: *If you need help, reach out and get it.* The emotional-health industry is available now more than ever before. Find a counselor, recruit a coach, meet with your spiritual teacher, or call a friend who will listen and be honest with you.

Asking for help is not a show of weakness; it's a sign of strength. Take the shame off what troubles you. Get it out of the darkness and into the light. Humans help humans. Not allowing

Asking for help is not a show of weakness; it's a sign of strength.

a friend or professional to help you isn't noble. It's a decision not to show up for the life allotted to you—and a disservice to this world and the people who love you. Think of these watchful souls as lifeguards, and reach out to one if your strategy has you stuck in a tide pool of pain. Choose to put yourself around others who can help you nurture a healthy perspective. You are worth it!

Whenever you move through painful seasons, well-meaning people who love you may have opinions about what's best for you. Just because someone has a suggestion doesn't mean you need to heed it. Remember, you get to process your emotions in a way that works for you. Lean into it if your process moves you forward and protects you against self-harm or sabotage.

Moving through a season of intense pain requires vigilance for remembering what you can and cannot control. Your resilience for maintaining healthy mindset patterns and your tolerance for the words and behaviors of others may weaken. That's normal. Remember, give yourself and others grace.

You'll also want to remind yourself that although you cannot change other people, you can change how their words and behavior land on you. You get to decide what you absorb and what you let roll off you like rain droplets on a waterproof jacket. You're in charge of—and 100 percent responsible—for how you engage your emotions.

You get to decide what you absorb and what you let roll off you like rain droplets on a waterproof jacket.

Anyone can show up in reaction to life like a toddler, throwing tantrums and blaming personal agony on others, events, or even themselves. Take a breath and remind yourself of the mature soul you've become.

Your evolved emotional state may shock others at first if they're used to getting a different reaction out of you. Stand firm. You are *not* in charge of their process of relating to your sadness; you control how you want to process your pain. It's ok to let others be themselves. Your healthy mindset isn't wrong; neither are the reactions of others. It's merely a shift because of a change in a previous pattern. Allow others time to settle into your new one.

It may not feel natural at first to bravely surf your pain waves, especially if you're used to getting stuck in tide pools. Ride it anyway. Your feelings will catch up to your cognitive choice. You'll grow into your decision to live according to how you want to feel, not how you are used to feeling or how you want others to respond.

Manipulating your behavior to achieve or avoid a reaction from others may have served you in the past. It may have even helped you get through rough patches. Your past behavior wasn't wrong. However, some of it won't serve you moving forward. Now you get to decide what you want and how you'll show up. Will you ride your pain waves or be crushed by them? Here are some questions that can help you reach the shore.

What is the truth surrounding my current situation?

_____

_____

_____

_____

What can I control about this situation or life event?

_____

_____

_____

_____

What can I not control?

_____

_____

_____

_____

What narrative surrounding this painful season am I telling myself?

_____

_____

_____

_____

How does this story make me feel? Do I feel natural pain or am I stuck in emotional misery?

_____

_____

_____

_____

Is this the best story for my situation or could I weave a more empowering, truthful story?

_____

_____

Am I telling my story from an abundance mindset or a scarcity mindset?

_____

_____

Have I given another person or event ownership of my emotions?

_____

_____

Have I given a disempowering story control over my moods?

_____

_____

How will I take back my power to control how I feel today?

_____

_____

_____

_____

(For help creating a better story, revisit the exercise from Chapter 4.)

PRACTICE PEACE

My friend, Claudia, with bold and authentic words, describes heavy grief over parting with her fifteen-year-old son, Will. She writes, *"You were and continue to be one of the greatest joys of my life. Perhaps the loss of you physically here allows me to experience that joy even more—and savor the dark side of it too. It's an ache that surrenders only for a while—and I welcome its return. If it eases up for too long I yearn for it—a reminder you were here. It's a space that need not be occupied by comfort, nor turned into a lesson, but rather exists as a remembrance of you."*[29]

Claudia is in touch with her pain. She knows the power of her waves and rides them bravely. She faces the changing tide and embraces the truth that her waves will continue to rise and calm. Claudia knows how to show up for life, even when it hurts tremendously. Because she faces pain instead of numbing it, my friend lives ready to notice and receive the beauty surrounding her circumstance.

Claudia is natural light, an inspiration to others. She knows peace. On her Caring Bridge page, she describes grief as, *"A tight rosebud that feels almost stubborn and harsh, thorns ready to draw blood. Allow it to open, however, and there is a sweetness to it. A softness to the petals that makes you want to bury your face in its scent and inhale deeply."*

> **Peace bravely feels the rush of all emotions.**

Peace exemplifies living all in. Sometimes thought of as only calm, peace bubbles and overflows with abundance. Peace bravely feels the rush of all emotions. My God says in Isaiah 66:12, "I will extend peace to her like a river, and the wealth of nations like a flooding stream."

Living peacefully amid pain is beautiful. Peace flows. It is a "flooding stream," allowing the fluidity of your emotions to rise and fall.

Remember, rivers are not always or often calm. They're ever-changing—wild, unpredictable, and scary. In parts, they're quiet. Rivers keep moving, though. They flow forward, not backward.

My friend and pastor for twenty years, Steve Clifford, said it simply one Sunday, *"If everything were always perfect, there would be no reason for hope."*[30] In Matthew 5:4, Jesus spoke forward-minded words of hope: *"God blesses those who mourn, for they will be comforted."* And Psalms 34:18 (MSG) assures that *"If your heart is broken, you'll find God right there; if you're kicked in the gut, He'll help you catch your breath."*

> **You are not going under because you are not alone.**

Your creator loves you and is with you as you ride the painful waves of life. Ask your creator for help when fear and pain threaten to take your breath. Your divine will breathe into you and carry you through.

Your mighty creator goes with you through your messes and magnificence, through peaceful, slow-moving water and thunderous, harrowing waves. Come up for air, my friend, and inhale a deep, spirit-filled breath. You are not going under because you are not alone.

CHAPTER 12

EMBRACE YOUR POWER

"If you're brave enough to say goodbye,
life will reward you with a new hello."[31]

—PAULO COELHO

ay goodbye to fear and hello to a life you love. Motivational speaker Les Brown once said, *"Too many of us are not living our dreams because we are living our fears."*[32] It's time to change that.

Here's the spectacular deal: The power to love and live with bravery, instead of fear, is free, available, and accessible—in *all* circumstances. I know this because 2 Timothy 1:7 tells me, *"For God has not given us a Spirit of fear and timidity, but of power, love, and self-discipline."*

This verse tells me that the opposite of fear is power, love, and self-discipline—and the ability to live that way is already in me! (Not on my merit, though, thank goodness.) *The Spirit living in me is my power source.* I can say goodbye to the ravages of fear in my life because my God's Spirit has given me a brave heart.

> *How do you live in the great wide open with a brave heart? For starters, pay attention to what-ifs.*

A supernatural strength lives in you too! So, how do you release the power within you? How do you live in the great wide open with a brave heart? For starters, pay attention to what-ifs. I'll use my own experience to demonstrate what I mean. One night during the first week of the COVID-19 shelter-in-place, I felt anxious. My husband asked a simple question that propelled me to change my perspective: "Chris, what are you anxious about?"

In pondering how to answer him, I realized that my feelings stemmed from *what-ifs*. *What if* life never returns to the way it was? *What if* I get sick? *What if* my family gets sick? *What if* people lose their jobs? *What if* businesses close? *What if* the economy tanks? *What if* people die? *What if* I die? *What if, what if, what if?* Those two words are exhausting!

Sure, there were new unknowns when the pandemic hit. And there were many unknowns before the pandemic. Did I know when my loved ones or I would die, or what tomorrow held before COVID? I did not. The *what-ifs* I was fearing were outside of my control. Things happen and will continue to happen.

That night, I grabbed a notebook and started listing the things I could control: *my thoughts, what I ate, my energy, my beliefs, my words, my actions, what I read, what I watched, what I listened to, how I managed my time, how I prayed, and so forth.* The anxious thoughts left me as I wrote my list, and serenity filled their space.

Your fear during a crisis will not change the situation. However, your serenity during confusion will change how you show up for a crisis—and encourage those around you to stay calm. If you already have a problem, adding fear to that problem is just layering on a

> *If you already have a problem, adding fear to that problem is just layering on a second problem.*

second problem. The more you layer, the more anxious, brain-fogged, and unable to problem-solve you get. *Who needs that?* There is far greater power in layering on serenity and calmness instead.

Problems happen. You face them with power when you remember you already have everything you need in each moment to keep showing up and moving forward. Showing up for life, even when it's scary, demands bravery. And bravery makes you feel alive. So, think about your present situation and ask yourself:

How will I feel when I shift my focus to this moment and what I can control?

_____

_____

_____

_____

What is great about the present moment?

_____

_____

_____

_____

What have I gained since the event I once feared?

_____

_____

_____

_____

What can I do right now that will benefit others and myself six to twelve months from now?

_____

_____

_____

_____

Shifting your focus from what you cannot control to what you can manage will save unnecessary and unproductive anxiousness.

Depending on the life event, sadness or grief may remain. That's ok. You can let these emotions in most productively once fear clears out. Shifting your focus from what you cannot control to what you can manage will save unnecessary and unproductive anxiousness.

QUESTION YOUR FEAR

You have the power to question your fear when *what-ifs* bombard you. Take a moment right now and ask yourself:

What if my fear comes true? What do I believe will happen?

_____

_____

_____

Is that true? Will that happen?

_____

_____

What is the worst that could happen if my fear becomes a reality? (Picture the actual worst, not the imagined worst.)

_____

_____

_____

Live for the dream, not the nightmare.

If you're a "plan for the worst, hope for the best" type of thinker, make sure the "worst" you're preparing for is a viable outcome and not a dramatized tragedy. Preparation is excellent; however, preparing for an imagined disaster may cause you to cast a false vision. (Remember, when you focus on what you don't want to happen, you increase the chances of that thing happening! Live for the dream, not the nightmare.)

Next, ask yourself:

What if my fear comes true, and I change for the better? How will I be changed? How will I grow from this, either immediately or over time?

_____

_____

_____

_____

If applicable, how will my loved ones grow from this?

_____

_____

_____

What if my fear doesn't come true? How did I give away my energy toward something that never happened?

_____

_____

_____

_____

What will that spent energy cost me? What will it cost the people I love?

_____

_____

_____

_____

In 1948 C. S. Lewis wrote an essay in response to what much of the world feared most—the atomic bomb. Here's my favorite part of the essay:

> *"If we are all going to be destroyed by an atomic bomb, let that bomb, when it comes, find us doing sensible and human things—praying, working, teaching, reading, listening to music, bathing the children,*

playing tennis, chatting to our friends over a pint and a game of darts—not huddled together like frightened sheep and thinking about bombs. They may break our bodies (a microbe can do that), but they need not dominate our minds."[33]

Choose a peaceful mindset when difficult things rear their ugly heads.

There have always been, and continue to be, real threats to your way of life and survival. You'll be most effective in standing against any common enemy—be it a bomb, pandemic, terrorist, or tragedy—when you refuse to give that threat the power to control your mind and emotions.

Scary things happen. Choose a peaceful mindset when difficult things rear their ugly heads. By maintaining a focused and meaningful attitude, you choose powerful, effective action over weak, ineffective fear.

Here's how one of my clients worked through some of her fears.

Lily: Chris, I'm so afraid for my daughter, Maddie. She's heading out on her first deployment next week. I'm having trouble sleeping and feel shaky and panicked. I don't know how to live this way for the next nine months of her deployment.

Me: You said you're afraid for your daughter. What are you afraid of, Lily?

Lily: My baby girl is heading into the most dangerous situation I can think of. I'm afraid of all of it.

Me: Describe "all of it." What are you afraid of exactly?

Lily: Well, the biggest is that she'll get hurt.

Me: Is your daughter getting hurt your biggest fear?

Lily: No, I'm afraid she'll die.

Me: Great honesty, Lily. Is serving during deployment the only way Maddie can die?

Lily: No. The odds stacked against her are way higher, though!

Me: Is that true, or is it possible there has always been a likelihood of Maddie getting hurt or even dying?

Lily: I've been afraid of my kids getting hurt or dying since they were born. Military deployment is just scarier!

Me: What makes this situation scarier than the first time Maddie left the hospital in a moving vehicle or got her driver's permit?

Lily: My daughter being in the military isn't how life should be. A mother shouldn't have to watch her baby ship out overseas. Maddie shouldn't be in this situation!

Me: I understand this is scary for you. Is this also scary for Maddie?

Lily: No way! That crazy girl is watching her childhood dream play out! She's excited.

Me: What's the difference between your perspective of Maddie's deployment and her perspective of it?

Lily: The difference is Maddie anticipated her military job and all it requires. I believed it shouldn't happen. I saw her joining the military as inviting unwanted chaos, so I hated it. I can't, no, in the past, I couldn't (good job Lily for choosing more valid words) see why someone would want to create more danger and problems for themselves. I get it now. This job is not a problem for Maddie. Just for me.

Me: Excellent, Lily! Way to go! So what about Maddie's deployment can you not control?

Lily: I cannot control what Maddie loves and wants to do. I cannot control who Maddie is or how she chooses to serve during her lifetime. I've been able to protect Maddie from many harmful things during her life; however, I've never had complete control over all things that could harm her.

Me: Excellent. So, what can you control?

Lily: My perspective! My emotions. I can control my habits and daily routine for sure. I can meditate and pray first thing in the morning instead of turning on the news. I can also control my focus. I've been allowing myself to focus on all the things that could happen to Maddie, making me feel sick. Now that I think of it, I've concentrated on impossible things happening. The more I let my focus wander, the more dramatic and imaginative it gets!

Me: Fantastic, Lily! Keep making lists of what you can and cannot control to lock this mindset—choosing a focus that serves you will become your new pattern. Now, what's great about Maddie's deployment?

Lily: Maddie is thriving in a career in line with her wiring. And she's deploying with some of her best friends. Modern technology is great too. I'll be able to text and talk to Maddie often, which will be calming for me.

Me: Great! So, is it true that you have to live with the fearful feelings you described over the next nine months of Maddie's deployment?

Lily: No. I already feel much less afraid. Now I'm confident my fear won't take me down. I know I'm smart enough to look at any situation that scares me for what it truly is instead of what I think it should be or instead of imagining it is something worse.

Lily chose to stop living her fears. She decided to celebrate that her daughter was living her dreams. She chose to take back her own life by embracing love, self-discipline, and the divine power residing within her. She decided to live with bravery.

Remember, the power to love and live with bravery—instead of fear—is free, available, and accessible in *all* circumstances. Begin by connecting with your spiritual self. Then, follow the wisdom of C.S. Lewis. Say goodbye to fear and hello to living your dreams. Celebrate your life by doing sensible and human things. Lead with love. Live with self-discipline. Your dreams will follow your brave, rational, and beautifully human heart.

Say goodbye to fear and hello to living your dreams.

CHAPTER 13

FLIP YOUR EXPECTATIONS

"Things turn out best for those who make
the best of the way things turn out."[34]

—JOHN WOODEN

Unmet expectations can drive you cuckoo—if you let them. So, don't let them! Get curious about them instead. It's the path to peace and a more powerful mindset.

Remember Lily? She expected her daughter Maddie to look at life through the same lens she does. Lily thrives in a secure environment. And that's great! It's how her creator wired her.

Maddie's higher power wired her for adventure. Risk doesn't make her feel fearful; it makes her feel alive and focused. Serving in the military is Maddie's path to showing up for a life she loves.

When Lily realized she had tied her fears about Maddie's career choice to her own expectations and personal wiring, she could finally exhale instead of holding her breath and expecting the worst. Instead of viewing things through the clouded lens of her expectations, Lily's curiosity enabled her to take a deep breath and see things as they were.

With practice, Lily has learned to flip her expectations and

Are you ready to trade cuckoo for curiosity, peace, and a more joyful mindset?

celebrate that Maddie is living the way her creator wired her. Lily also discovered that life wraps some of its greatest gifts differently than expected. She's traded cuckoo for curiosity, and the flip has given her peace and a more joyful mindset.

Are you ready to trade cuckoo for curiosity, peace, and a more joyful mindset? Here's an exercise to help you get started.

First, think about an event or circumstance that made you feel fearful, disappointed, or even a bit cuckoo. Now, ask yourself:

Was my reaction because of an expectation that didn't go how I imagined it would?

_____

_____

What was my expectation?

_____

_____

What's great about how it did go?

_____

_____

_____

What's a better interpretation of the event?

_____

_____

_____

What's there to appreciate about the situation?

_____

_____

_____

Curiosity creates a powerful mental and emotional reset that demonstrates self-love and self-discipline. Your brain sends your body a message to alert you to pause and recognize when a lousy thought or question goes

Getting curious when expectations get whacked is invigorating!

through your mind so you can flip it to a better one. *Incredible, right?* Getting curious when expectations get whacked is invigorating!

DEVELOP YOUR FLIP MUSCLE

For years, a question floated like pond scum through my subconscious: *How can I be noticed and appreciated in this situation?* Once I realized that question was stifling my joy, I flipped it this way: *What will I notice and appreciate in this situation?* That flip changed my life. My relationships are richer now, and my happiness is no longer dependent on things outside my control. I get to control my joy!

Here are some more flips that can make a huge difference in the way you view your life and expectations:

- *Who is loving me in this situation?*
  Flip to *Who will I love in this situation?*

- *How am I being appreciated?*
  Flip to *Whom and what do I appreciate?*

- *How can I be understood?*
  Flip to *How can I understand?*

With that mindset, use the following exercise to help you develop your flip muscle:

Think of the last time you had an unmet expectation. Take a second and get a specific example in mind. Then, ask yourself:

Was I seeking to be consoled, understood, or loved? Was I expecting to receive something or be pardoned?

_____

_____

Now, think of that same situation through a flipped lens of seeking to console, understand, or love. Imagine that you gave something or pardoned someone else instead. Notice the expectation flip and ask yourself:

How do I feel now?

_____

_____

_____

_____

Next, ask yourself:

What current situation in my life could use an expectation flip?

_____

_____

How will that adjustment contribute to my contentment?

_____

_____

_____

_____

How will it enhance my enjoyment of what I have?

_____

_____

_____

_____

Remember, you don't have to believe the words at first to flip them. Your beliefs and feelings will follow. Condition your new way of managing expectations like a muscle at the gym. You don't walk out of the first workout looking like your end goal. Condition, repeat, and create new patterns.

You get to choose how you feel— regardless of other people.

Flipping your expectations will empower you to feel how you decide you want to feel. Your creator gifted you with invigorating free will. Your power to choose your opinions and thoughts is a privilege. Remember, it's every person's right to decide how to think and feel—about you, others, politics, anything. It's your right to determine how that lands on you. You get to choose how you feel—regardless of other people.

EXPECT THE BEAUTY OF THE UNEXPECTED

Forrest Gump's mama taught him this truth: *"Life was like a box of chocolates. You never know what you're gonna get."*[35] So, in the big-picture scheme of things, think about the beautiful and not-so-beautiful unexpected and ask yourself:

What would happen if I expected meaningful chaos?

_____

_____

_____

_____

What if I anticipated a day of attaching powerful interpretations to whatever happens?

_____

_____

_____

_____

What if I expected and appreciated the unexpected?

_____

_____

_____

What if I spent more energy seeking thankfulness for what is rather than expectation of what is not?

_____

_____

_____

_____

What if I started each day by giving it to my higher power instead of following my own agenda?

_____

_____

_____

_____

What if my higher power took away my illusion of control over the future so I would lean into divine trust more completely? What would I entrust to my creator?

_____

_____

_____

_____

Your joy is yours to control. Celebrate that! Your life is yours to live fully as your creator wired you.

Here's a simple, life-giving prayer that will help you launch each day of your beautiful life with power, love, and self-discipline. It is a prayer

Your joy is yours to control.

that will help you flip expectations and, by doing so, empower you to show up for the life you want to live with a tender, curious, and joyful heart.

"... O Divine Master,

Grant that I may not so much seek to be consoled as to console;

To be understood, as to understand;

To be loved, as to love;

For it is in giving that we receive.

It is in pardoning that we are pardoned,

And it is in dying that we are born to Eternal Life.

Amen."[36]

CHAPTER 14

DO THE HARD STUFF

"He who has a Why to live for can bear almost any How."[37]

—FRIEDRICH NIETZSCHE

You are smarter than you think. And tougher than you know. That's why you can and get to do something challenging every day. Something hard that propels you in the direction you want to go. Something that makes you sweat, or shiver, a bit. (Maybe a lot.)

As your life coach, I'm not issuing an Olympic-sized edict; you don't have to scale a mountain every twenty-four hours. However, to live the life you want, you must push obstacles out of your way—stretching your mind, body, and spirit over chasms that keep you stuck *here* when you want to be, well, *over there.*

Bottom line? Living the life you want takes grit—grinding it out even when your muscles are screaming, "Uncle!" Grit is a choice that leads to mental toughness.

Hebrews 12:11-13 gets down to it, *"No discipline is enjoyable while it is happening—it's pain-*

Living the life you want takes grit—grinding it out even when your muscles are screaming, "Uncle!"

ful! But afterward there will be a peaceful harvest of right living for those who are trained in this way. So take a new grip with your tired hands and strengthen your weak knees. Mark out a straight path for your feet so that those who are weak and lame will not fall but become strong."

Know this: Getting where you want to go will catapult you out of your comfort zone. And that's a good thing. Growth happens when you pop your bubble wrap.

Growth happens when you pop your bubble wrap.

I've ended my morning showers with a cold, two-minute blast for years. *It sucks.* And then I feel alive. Even more than the physical and mental health benefits of cold therapy (reduced inflammation, increased metabolism, improved immune response) this ritual keeps me in a pattern of taking difficult action. Thus far, there hasn't been one morning when I've thought, *Fantastic; I get to have a cold blast now.* Instead, I grit my teeth, turn off the hot water, and take the cold—knowing that the results are worth it!

Here's an exercise that can help you discover the great world outside your comfort zone. Ask yourself:

Am I willing to do something to step out of my comfort zone each day to experience growth? If not, what's holding me back?

What things do I do that suck at the moment yet push me outside my comfort zone and make me feel alive?

_____

_____

_____

Am I celebrating myself for these actions, or have I mistaken them for things that cause unnecessary stress or anxious feelings?

_____

_____

What will serve me best to move forward—doing the hard thing anyway, or avoiding it?

_____

_____

How will I change my perspective to see difficult actions as embracing growth rather than stress producers?

_____

_____

Before you panic, thinking you might run yourself right off a cliff when doing hard things, *relax*. You have a built-in safety net—natural survival instincts that move you away from what's dangerous or harmful for you. Pay attention and differentiate what actions or behaviors are best to avoid vs. which ones you would rather avoid because they are, well, sucky hard.

When tempted to avoid, procrastinate, or quit, ask yourself, *Is what I'm resisting going to move me in the direction I want to go, or not?* Resistance signals growth is near. If it moves you forward, do it even if your first inclination is to resist. Celebrate that you're one step closer to living your life all in where you want to be instead of languishing where you are. Embrace discomfort as fuel to get you going rather than allowing fear to immobilize you. Know that feeling anxious is part of being human. If you work to avoid it at all costs, you're erasing an instinct meant to guide you to your field of dreams.

Embrace discomfort as fuel to get you going rather than allowing fear to immobilize you.

An important reality check: *If you experience debilitating worry or panic, acknowledge those feelings.* It could signal a pattern of unease triggered by things you need to recognize. Check your focus and story using what you've learned from previous chapters.

Feeling anxious is human. Living all in includes getting curious about your emotions instead of ignoring or erasing them. You can't erase unsettled feelings; however, you can learn to dance with them because you're smart and tough.

Summon the courage to embrace hard conversations with a caring mental health partner who can help you bring what's triggering your anxious feelings to the surface—where you can manage them well. Remember, you get to be in charge of beautiful you, so don't hesitate to invest in counseling that can help free you of gunk that's holding you back.

VISUALIZE YOUR RESULTS

When working with high performers, I've noticed a tendency to ditch the entire goal when things aren't going well. It's tempting to want things perfect—or not at all. If this sounds like you, great news—that's ok! It's part of how you're wired. And when used to your advantage, your tendency toward the extreme fuels your success.

You don't have to plateau, get stuck, quit, or move backward because one approach didn't work. Use your energy as fuel to get where you want to go rather than wasting it on frustration, being overwhelmed, anger, or sadness. Don't ditch the goal. Ditch that one tactic that bombed and strategize a different one.

Here's the deal: *Doing the hard stuff to reach a goal includes knowing when to tweak tactics to achieve the desired result instead of ditching the plan altogether.* Doing the hard stuff well is simple: Keep strategies that work, scrap the ones that don't, shake off failures, adjust, and continue moving forward. Successful people usually do more things that don't work than work on their way to the desired result.

Welcome mistakes. Welcome imperfection. Welcome redos.

There's a slight shift between being almost to a goal and arriving at that goal. You may have heard this referred to as a two-millimeter shift. You may live ninety-eight percent of the life you want. You have great results, which is where comfort can set in. To have extraordinary results, go for the extra two percent! Don't stop. Welcome mistakes. Welcome imperfection. Welcome redos. Tweak the tactics. Hold fast to your end goal. Peak athletic performers know that getting better and going to a higher level of ability requires getting worse for some time to refine a skill.

Here are some questions to ask yourself as you go for the extra two percent:

What in my life requires my persistence to refine instead of pause?

_____

_____

_____

_____

What outcomes do I want in the next thirty days? Three months? Six months? One year? Five years?

_____

_____

_____

_____

With those refinements in mind, use the following exercise to set goals, starting with your thirty-day goal:

1. Think Result

You can use this exercise for long- or short-term goals. A thirty-day plan is a simple one to launch your new practice. Write down your thirty-day goal. You can call this your result, outcome, target, objective, holy grail, or whatever word excites you most. To achieve your result, you must think clearly about what you want. To write a clear goal, use the SMART[38] acronym. Here's how:

Specific: Clearly define your particular goal. Set a specific outcome.

Measurable: Qualify an indicator of progress. How will you know when you've achieved your goal? What will you notice?

Assignable: Specify who will do what to reach the outcome.

Realistic: Your goal is realistic to you, even if it isn't to others, given your available resources, knowledge, and time. It is actionable and attainable.

Time-Defined: Set a specific date you'll achieve this by, not merely a timeframe.

Here's how my client, Anna, presented her SMART thirty-day goal:

Anna: My SMART goal is to convert the guest bedroom in my house to office space by March 30th.

Me: Great! Your goal is *specific* (convert bedroom to office space). Now let's check if it's *measurable*. How will you know your guest room is an office space?

Anna: I'll know because my desk, computer, and file drawers will replace the bedroom set. And the clutter I've been storing there will be gone.

Me: Super! (Anna must get even more specific about her goal to measure it.) Specifically, what clutter?

Anna: There are four unpacked boxes in the closet of that room. I haven't opened them since I moved to this house three years ago, so I know I don't need most of what's in them. I will see the clutter is gone when the four boxes are out of the room and when I go through the nightstands and clear out the papers I've been tossing in there. It's all old receipts and things I thought I might need one day.

Me: Excellent! We'll come back to this clutter and have a plan for where it goes exactly. For now, getting it out of the room is measurable success toward your goal. Is this goal *assignable*?

Anna: Yes. I know who to recruit to help me. I have the resources and resourcefulness needed to accomplish this task.

Me: Is it *realistic* to you?

Anna: Yes. My sister says I'll never do it. Haha! The goal is realistic and attainable.

Me: And I know it's *time-defined* since you gave me a date of March 30th. You've got yourself a SMART goal, Anna!

2. Determine *Why You Want Your Result*

The next step is to write down *why* you want your result. This step comes second for two critical reasons. First, you must know what you want. (Remember what you learned in Chapter Two.) Then, associate with why you want what you want before moving into strategy.

If you're a high achiever, you may be tempted to skip this step (and possibly step one) so you can develop your strategy. You love lists and getting stuff done. However, it's vital that you first know your desired outcome. Know the reasons *why* you want what you want, second. Reaching goals is about eighty percent mindset and twenty percent strategy. Your mindset is the emotion and heart behind *why* you want the results you do. It will drive you.

> *Associate with why you want what you want before moving into strategy.*

Here's how Anna got her *Why*:

Me: Alright, Anna, get into a distraction-free place. Inhale. Exhale. Close your eyes. Now visualize yourself on your goal date. It's March 30th, and you're walking into your converted office space. Be there as if it's your reality right now. See it, feel it, breathe it in, hear it. Now, sink into that moment even deeper, staying there for the remainder of this exercise.

(Anna is now in a productive state of body and mind. She's out of the confusion of her head and ready to lead and goal-set from her heart).

Anna: Ok, it's March 30th, and I'm walking into my new office.

Me: What do you notice? What do you see? How does the room sound? Smell? How do you feel walking into the room?

Anna: I can see the floor! And out the window! I had always kept the blinds shut to hide the mess. Now, it's light and open. And it smells fresh! No more musky dust smell. I smell the eucalyptus oil in the infuser on my desk. I hear the stillness. I can hear myself think!

Me: You're doing fantastic! Stay in this moment. And how do you feel?

Anna: (Her voice cracking) I feel light. And free. (She teared up a little bit, and there was a pause in her description). I feel productive. Like a badass boss lady! I feel clear-minded and energized. I'm ready to take on the world, or at least my world.

Me: And what does this mean to your world?

Anna: (Her voice still a bit crackly) This was more than a workspace. This room created space in my life. Space for my relationships with friends and family. Space for my art and creativity to flourish. Space to work. Space to breathe. Space for me. And the lightness I feel in my spirit will lead to lightness in my body. I know I'll achieve my desired weight now, no doubt. Oh my gosh, I see now that all my other goals hinged on this one. I was distracted from getting this room cleared because I thought other things took priority.

Me: Amazing, Anna! Let's pause to get these feelings on paper while they are fresh.

Now is an excellent time to pause and record your visualization experience. While you visualize your future achieved moment as if it were right now, grab your pen and ask yourself:

How do I feel at this moment? (Write down all the feelings that accomplishing this goal has brought you.)

_____

_____

_____

_____

What does my life look like now that I have accomplished this result?

_____

_____

_____

_____

Be thorough and specific in your description of what accomplishing this goal looks like in your life. Ask yourself:

What am I wearing?

_____

_____

Where am I living?

_____

_____

Who am I with?

_____

_____

How do I feel?

_____

_____

_____

What do I see?

_____

_____

What do I hear?

_____

_____

What do I eat?

_____

_____

What are my daily rituals?

_____

_____

_____

What does this mean to me and others I care about and who care about me?

_____

_____

_____

_____

Get it all on paper. This is your *Why*—the reason you must achieve your goal!

3. *Strategize*

Now that you know *what* you want and *why* you want it, you're ready to strategize. Yay! Once Anna had an established smart goal and a why, here's how I helped her come up with her strategy:

> **Me:** All right, Anna, outstanding job so far! Now, close your eyes, breathe deep, and get back to your visualization of March 30th. Your new, fresh workspace is perfect. You're feeling light, clear-minded and productive. (Note: Play with what works best for you to get into your visualization—eyes open or shut, standing or sitting. Whatever posture works best for you to be in your moment is the one to use.)
>
> **Anna:** Ok, I'm there.

Me: Tell me what steps you took to get to this moment. What did you do specifically to make this fabulous room happen?

Anna: I listed the bedroom set for sale online. I found a buyer who would haul it away. I cleared out the nightstand papers.

Me: What did you do with the papers? (This detail is important to the strategy.)

Anna: I went through them, tossed the unnecessary, and filed what I needed.

Me: How long did this take, and what day did you set aside? (Get specific. Schedule a time, date, and place to complete the actions necessary to achieve your end goal.)

Anna: Tuesday. I created new file folders for papers that didn't have a home. And I set aside three hours.

Me: Great! Go on. What else did you do to get to this magical moment on March 30th?

Anna: I got a friend to help me move my desk, chair, and file drawers from my garage into the room. I moved the four boxes from the closet into the garage. I went through them one box at a time. I sorted their contents into keep, toss, and giveaway piles.

Me: How long did this take, and what day did you do it?

Anna: Wednesday. It took all day. About eight hours. I took the giveaway items to a donation station in that timeframe.

Me: What did you do with the "keep" items?

Anna: There were not a lot of keep items in the boxes. Each one had a place it belonged, so those were easy to put away once I separated them into their pile.

Me: Great! What else did you do to make this goal happen?

Anna: I bought an oil infuser and nice-smelling oils for the room. I took a day to dust, vacuum, wash the windows, and clean the light fixture.

Me: Terrific strategy, Anna! Take another deep breath, open your eyes, and let's record what you just said. This list of action items is your strategy.

You'll strategize best after you've emotionally connected to your why and all the feelings that achieving your goal will bring you.

I record the strategy of clients as they visualize their results. You can record as you strategize. The idea is that your best ideas for strategic actions toward your goal will come to you when you're in *heart space*, not *headspace*. You'll strategize best after you've emotionally connected to your why and all the feelings that achieving your goal will bring you.

As you visualize the future result you want, ask yourself,

What did I do to get to this moment?

_____

_____

Write down everything you did to achieve this goal. List all the specific actions you took to get here as they come to you. You'll organize these action items later; get them on paper first.

Ask yourself:

What did I do to get here that was a real challenge? What else?

_____

_____

_____

_____

Write it all down. Now you have a list—a strategy. You can organize this list however works most efficiently for you. Keep the action items specific. For example, if you wrote, _have morning meditation each day_, then add what time of day and how long you will meditate. Schedule your to-do's. Write down when, with whom, and where you will take these actions.

Before moving to the next action item, celebrate each time you check something off your list—schedule time to celebrate and acknowledge yourself before charging on to the next task. Celebrating can be a moment of patting yourself on the back, time with a friend, or a unique excursion for yourself. Celebrate in a manner meaningful to you each time you step closer to your goal.

You are ready to get results! Test this exercise with different-sized goals and various timelines. Some strategy lists will be longer than others. Using this system, you can create your six-month to five-year plans and then break the strategy sections down into individual attainable goals.

For example, if you set a goal that you'll publish a book in one year, you write it as a SMART goal, visualize yourself having already published the book, and (while in that future visualization) record your *why*. Then list the actions necessary to get the book published.

The strategy list of action items may seem long since it includes all the things you'll do in the next year to accomplish the goal of publishing the book. However, take just one item from the list, let's say it's to *find a cover designer* and you'll make that action into a SMART goal and use the system to get your *why* and *strategy* down for finding a cover designer. This approach makes the process productive and manageable—and creates opportunities for celebration along the way to the end goal.

Remember, you are smarter than you think. And tougher than you know.

The more you use this system, the more comfortable you'll become at adapting it to work best for you. Tweak the tactics. Use what works and dump the rest. The idea is to set goals without skipping any of the three steps **in this order:**

1. Know your *SMART goal*;
2. Visualize and record your *why*;
3. *Strategize* your specific action items.

Remember, you are smarter than you think. And tougher than you know. You can do something hard, something challenging, every day. And you will because you are you.

CHAPTER 15

RECOGNIZE WHAT SHIMMERS

"Beware lest you lose the substance
by grasping at the shadow."[39]

—AESOP

Driven achievers often focus on what's missing instead of what they already have. It can lead to leaving the eighty percent of what's shimmering to seek the twenty percent perceived as lacking.

Philosopher Aesop focused on this precarious tendency in his fable, "The Dog and the Shadow." A dog crossing a bridge with juicy meat in its mouth sees its shadow in the water below. When the dog opens his mouth to take the shadow meat, he loses the succulent meal in his mouth. Aesop called this "grasping at the shadow," and this tendency has led to poor judgment calls for centuries.[40]

When I work with an individual or couple looking to end a relationship, I first ask my clients to write down everything they love or used to love about the other person—everything that drew them to that individual. In a separate list, I ask them to write down everything they wish were different about that person; everything they perceive is missing.

More times than not, the list of what they love (the stuff that shimmers) far outweighs the list of what's missing; the great substance easily dominates the thin shadow. Yet people will often leave what's great to make up for the lack. The tragedy is, even if they do find that missing twenty percent, they've settled for twenty percent great—when the great used to be eighty percent.

When you leave what's excellent in search of the ideal, you'll end up short.

Don't get hung up on the numbers I'm using here. I use percentages to illustrate that when you leave what's excellent in search of the ideal, you'll end up short.

Here are simple questions to check your focus, so you don't grasp at shadows and lose your substance:

In what area of my life do I feel dissatisfied?

_____

_____

With this area in mind, create two lists:

1. What do I believe is great?

_____

_____

2. *What do I believe is lacking?*

Initiate a ritual of reciting your positives at least once when you wake and once before you go to sleep.

Now, focus on the list of greats instead of the lackings. Recite this list aloud. Place it where you can read it several times a day. Practice shifting your focus to this positive list repeatedly until your focus naturally goes there first instead of to what's missing.

As with any skill you want to enhance, repetition and consistency are vital. Initiate a ritual of reciting your positives at least once when you wake and once before you go to sleep. (Remember, it takes time to change old focus patterns and establish new ones.) With time, you'll focus primarily on the things that serve and move you forward instead of getting stuck in thoughts about lack.

If your list of negatives is longer than positives, investigate why. Bounce it off a coach, counselor, or mentor. Maybe a change is best; however, make your two lists first. That way, you'll change from the mindset of a grateful acknowledgment of what you have and thoughtful consideration of what you want, rather than from a desperate desire to escape in search of something better.

Make sure you absorb this core truth: *The exercise isn't about settling for what you have. It's about not settling for a romanticized, false alternative. It's about appreciating what you already have as you decide when, how, and if to change it.*

I did this exercise with my client, Susan, founder and CEO of a successful florist company. As a high-achieving entrepreneur, Susan came to coaching to take her business to the next level. She had shops in several Midwest locations and wanted to expand to the East and West Coasts.

During our weekly sessions, Susan would usually mention her

husband, Jared, as a side note to the business topic at hand. I learned that Jared and Susan had gotten to a point in their thirty-four-year marriage where they existed as friendly roommates rather than an intimate couple. They even slept in separate bedrooms. Curious, I asked Susan to tell me more about their relationship. She was hesitant and didn't know what it had to do with her entrepreneurial aspirations; however, she obliged me.

I gave Susan the assignment of writing down everything she fell in love with about her husband and all the reasons she was excited to marry Jared thirty-four years earlier. Here's how our session following the assignment played out:

Susan: Jared was funny. We laughed a lot. Jared was spontaneous. He made me feel special and sexy. We flirted and had strong physical attraction. We could also talk for hours about nothing in particular. We just enjoyed one another's company.

Me: What changed?

Susan: Life happened. Kids happened. Careers happened. Once the kids were grown and gone, we started working longer hours. Jared is an attorney. He's excellent at his job and buried himself in his work once the kids left.

Me: And you buried yourself in your work?

Susan: Yes! The business is thriving. I hired you to continue growing my business and take it to the next level.

Me: You said life changed; kids and careers happened. Did Jared also lose the characteristics you fell in love with?

Susan: Yes. He's no longer funny, spontaneous, or flirty. He doesn't make me feel sexy or special. Not only do we not talk for hours, we barely talk for minutes. We've become comfortable with our relationship this way.

Me: Are you certain Jared no longer possesses those great original characteristics?

Susan: Yes, I'm sure. And we haven't been intimate in over two years. That's the problem.

Me: Is it possible that Jared didn't change and that only your life circumstances changed?

Susan: No, Jared changed.

Me: Humor me. Imagine for a moment that Jared is still funny, spontaneous, and flirty. Imagine your relationship the way it was when you first fell in love.

Susan: (smiles) Well, that would be great!

Me: Imagine it *is* great, and those things you loved about Jared and how you felt around him are still alive in your relationship.

Susan: Ok, but I don't know what this has to do with growing my business.

Me: Hang in there with me. Reset. Deep breath in for four counts. Now out for four counts.

Susan: (Deep exhale) All right, I'm imagining it.

Me: Great! In this image, how are you feeling?

Susan: Epic! I feel confident, clear, and undistracted by life. Jared and I are a team that can do anything.

Me: You're doing great! Stay here. Tell me how you are interacting with Jared. How are you treating him?

Susan: Like my guy! I'm embarrassed to say it out loud, but I'll share that I'm *very* attracted to him.

Me: Susan, would you trust me with a different assignment than we've had in the past?

Susan: Sure.

Me: Excellent. For the next two weeks, interact with Jared as if he is "your guy," the man you fell in love with. No matter what Jared does or says, and no matter how you feel on a given day, keep coming back to the focus of the man you fell in love with.

Susan: He won't know what hit him. This will throw him for a loop.

Me: Good! We're interrupting an old pattern of focus and testing one that hasn't been active in years. Yes, it may throw him for a loop. Just stick with it for two weeks.

Susan: I'll do it, and it's going to be hard to treat him like my guy when he hasn't shown up as that guy in ages.

Me: Won't this be fun then!

Two weeks later, this was my conversation with Susan:

Susan: Well, the first few days were weird. It didn't feel natural to revisit those feelings. It felt like I was dating a stranger. I even planned a dinner date out for us. Jared seemed a little surprised and didn't say anything. I could tell he was curious and open to my new behavior. Then around day four, I could tell new patterns were forming. We were talking again after work. I made a point to coordinate sharing dinner times at home together since that's what we used to do in our early years. We started having morning coffee together again too. Jared's entire demeanor changed. He began to open up. And smile. He became pretty talkative during dinner time. This made me feel comfortable. We even had a few laughs. By the end of the two weeks, it felt like we were a couple again.

Me: So, is it true that your husband is no longer funny, spontaneous, and flirty?

Susan: Not true at all! Life changed. Jared has grown and changed in some ways. What's great, though, is the qualities I fell in love with actually didn't change! We both just forgot they were there. And what an ass I've been. I know I haven't been showing up for him as the woman he fell in love with either. I focused on the kids, then on work. I neglected to focus on the great stuff. I have been focused on the lousy twenty percent.

Me: So, what's your biggest takeaway from the assignment?

Susan: When I focus on the negatives, I see Jared in that unfair light. When I see him unfairly with twenty-percent vision, I act like the me I don't want to be. I act closed off—bitchy and controlling even. And when I act that way, he shuts down and doesn't feel safe to be his flirty, fun self. We've been stuck in a vicious cycle for years, both not showing up as the people we fell in love with. And I believe that has made us not love ourselves too.

Me: Great work, Susan! What will you do should your focus veer back to the lousy twenty percent?

Susan: Make my two lists and shift my focus!

Me: And is it possible you could use this exercise in your business since you're a pro at it now?

Susan: Yes! (Susan got uber-creative about how she could bring even more fun to her job and increase sales and morale by focusing more on what's worked and working rather than focusing on what isn't working.)

Update: Susan and Jared are sharing a bedroom again. Her business is growing steadily. Most of all, she's happy and allows her bright perspective to shine on others around her, causing them to shimmer too!

Your bright, shimmering light radiates the heck out of any dull spots. There's more abundance in you, your circumstances, and others than what's lacking. Recognize what shimmers and focus on those things rather than life's dimmers. All it requires is a conscious choice.

> *Recognize what shimmers and focus on those things rather than life's dimmers.*

CHAPTER 16

OWN YOUR PERSPECTIVE

"Live life as if everything is rigged in your favor."[41]

—RUMI

Grab a pen and write this statement on paper: *I get to choose how I interpret all situations.* Place it where you'll read it every day because this wisdom is life-changing!

Here's an example. When I had three teenagers living in our home, I often felt angry and out of control. I allowed their behaviors, attitudes, and body language to determine how I felt, thought, and behaved. On any given day, I would become infuriated. *Whew!*

One day, my life coach at the time told me, quite firmly, "Chris, your teenagers are not doing anything *to you!*"

Wow! That truth hit home. I had allowed the actions of three kids to orchestrate my reactions. When I realized my teenagers, along with their hormones, undeveloped brains, and *stellar* choices (and there were some doozies), weren't *making* me angry (because nobody has the power to do that), and that I was allowing myself to become angry in *reaction* to their actions, I shifted my mindset.

My teenagers didn't change; I did! I chose how I interpreted my situation. And as a calmer, non-reactive mom with a fresh

You get to choose how you interpret all situations and own your perspective.

perspective, I used my resourcefulness to lead myself and them forward. I went through my days bolstered by the belief that life wasn't happening *to me*; it was just happening—and happening in my favor. Huge difference!

Do you believe someone in your life is upsetting you? Here's a simple exercise to remind you that life happens, and you're in charge of your responses. You get to choose how you interpret all situations and own your perspective.

Ask yourself:

- Is this person doing something to me, or am I allowing myself to become upset?
- Does this individual hold power to upset me, or am I solely in charge of my emotions?
- What part of the situation can I control? What can I not control? (Write your responses to meld them into the physiology of your brain.)

Can Control: *Cannot Control:*

_____   _____

_____   _____

_____   _____

_____   _____

- What can I do with the part I can control?

- How will it benefit me to guard my emotions against reacting to another person or situation? How will I feel?

- How will I be able to interact with that person knowing I'm in control of my responses?

- Instead of allowing my emotions to escalate the interaction, what can I do instead to interrupt that old pattern/response? (Examples: take a walk outside, call someone, read or write for inspiration, pray, recite a verse, sing the lyrics to a song, do jumping jacks, count to ten, count backward from ten.)

Create options for yourself proactively so you're prepared to use them in the heat of any moment.

Create options for yourself proactively so you're prepared to use them in the heat of any moment. Play around with what works for you to interrupt old patterns of reaction when tempted.

Using physical movement to interrupt patterns will shut down the old response faster and most effectively by replacing it with something new at a physiological level. For example, if you choose to count backward from ten, count out loud and move your body or use hand motions instead of reacting. Jump up and down, spin around while you count. The more exaggerated (silly even) the physicality of your interruption, the quicker you'll be able to replace an old response with a better, more helpful one.

If you're in a space where flailing your body and using your outside voice isn't the best idea, you can still mentally shout and flail. Picture yourself vehemently interrupting the old pattern. This mental exercise will work since your mind doesn't know the difference between a strong visualization and reality. Remember, you alone choose how you interpret all situations. You are the master of your perspective!

THE ROAD UNRAVELED

And now for a reality check. Just because you have a passport to board a plane and travel to Thailand doesn't mean you won't encounter turbulence on your flight or an unexpected reroute to Bangladesh. As much as you can control your perspective, you cannot control all your circumstances. Though you can't always change how things go, you can change how you appreciate the way things went. Your relationship with your higher power comes into play here.

Though you can't always change how things go, you can change how you appreciate the way things went.

Author and pastor Steven Furtick nailed it when he said, *"Your perspective will either become your prison or your passport."*[42] Believing your life is happening for the good of a purpose beyond you is indeed the passport to the life you want to live.

The wisdom of Proverbs 16:9 teaches us, *"We can make our plans, but the Lord determines our steps."* When things don't go as planned, we can practice accepting that they're still going as our creator planned. Scripture counsels us to give thanks *in* all circumstances, not *for* all of them. My God doesn't call me to love all my circumstances. He calls me to walk with Him through them with a grateful heart.

For me, the words of 1 Thessalonians 5:16-18 (MSG) are light-filled guidance for keeping both the good days and the rocky ones in perspective: *"Be cheerful no matter what; pray all the time; thank God no matter what happens . . ."* I may not always understand my God's plan; however, I can always trust that there is a plan—and that His plan is best! Embracing this perspective as mine fills me with hope because I know my God will never abandon me and is always good even when circumstances are not. I've learned that what can feel like a destructive whirlwind is often a purge. Author Paul Coelho puts it this way: *"Not all storms come to disrupt your life; some come to clear your path."*[43]

To develop a purpose-driven perspective, get comfortable with life's incredible, ever-changing ebbs and flows. Developing such an outlook on life, especially during the hard times, takes practice, patience, and a lot of grace. Often, we must trust the process, even though it isn't fun, because it strengthens us for the future. An old Chinese proverb makes the truth about struggles visual: *"What the caterpillar calls the end of the world, the master calls the butterfly."*

Through good times and bad, I rest in the wisdom of Romans 8:28 (NIV): *"And we know that in all things God works for the good of those who love Him, who have been called according to his purpose."* This verse affirms me that all things work out according to God's purpose, not my own!

Leaning on divine strength will get you *through* difficulty, not out of it. And while we don't always know what's good for us, our higher power does. The adage made famous by Garth Brooks says it all: *"Some of God's greatest gifts are unanswered prayers."*

WATCH OUT FOR ROCKS

Time for another reality check: Other people will tip your boat, especially if you load their rocks in it. Since you get to choose how to interpret all situations, you'll want to teach yourself that helping others doesn't mean lugging their stuff.

You'll empower your loved ones best when you allow their refinement and growth to happen *for them*—through listening, love, and encouragement. Once again (because repetition creates good grooves in your brain), whatever a loved one is going through is not happening *to you*; it's most likely happening *for them*—and for you too.

Other people will tip your boat, especially if you load their rocks in it.

My client Paige's twenty-two-year-old son, Nathan, was living with her. He had just graduated from college when his father (Paige's ex-husband) died in a car crash. Here's a conversation Paige and I had six months after the accident:

Paige: I've had it with my son's laziness! He plays video games all day, making no effort to get a job, move out, and start his own life!

Me: Is that what you want for Nathan, moving out and making a life for himself?

Paige: Yes! That's what's best for him, and I want the best for my son. He worked so hard in college and had such lofty career ambitions until the crash.

Me: And what does he want?

Paige: I don't know. It appears he wants to stay in my house, eat my food, and use my television forever!

Me: Have you asked Nathan what he wants?

Paige: No.

Me: Why not?

Paige: I don't want to upset Nathan. His father only passed away six months ago, and I feel sad for him; they were so close. It breaks my heart to ask him to move out. The thought of it feels like I'm abandoning him, and he's already been through so much. As frustrating as his laziness is, I can't bear the thought of seeing him face more discomfort and transition.

Me: I understand you can't bear it. Can Nathan?

Paige: Probably. He's tough. Much tougher than I am. Yes, I believe he can bear it.

Me: If you asked Nathan what he wants, do you believe his answer would be to play video games in your house forever?

Paige: Ha! Absolutely not. He would want to move on by moving out. He would want to honor his father by making a life for himself.

Me*:* So why is he still living with you?

Paige: Why wouldn't he? He's got free rent, a live-in cook, a maid, and unlimited access to video games.

Me: So is catering to Nathan's laziness alleviating your fear of discomfort or his?

Paige: Oh, my. I've avoided encouraging Nathan to move forward or even discussing what he wants out of *my fear.*

Me: Are you willing to get out of your comfort zone for his benefit?

Paige: Hell, yes!

Me: Great! What can you say to Nathan to help him move forward?

In a previous session, Paige and I discussed the pain/pleasure principle and how change happens when the pain of staying the same exceeds the pain of changing, so I was thrilled when she made the following conclusion.

Paige: I can start by making my home less comfortable for him! I've created an environment where it's more painful for Nathan to look for a job than to play video games. I can make living with me more painful by unplugging the television and insisting Nathan does his share of the grocery shopping, cooking, yard work, and housework. I know, like a gentleman, he'll respect my wishes. I also know that he would think a job search was way more stimulating under those circumstances! (hard laughter from Paige).

Me: Excellent! And does making Nathan's current environment uncomfortable mean you're abandoning him?

Paige: It feels that way, but no. (Kudos to Paige for separating her feelings from the truth!)

Me: And does it mean you're hurting your son or his chance to show up for the future he wants?

Paige: Not at all! The opposite. It's the best way to love Nathan where he is right now.

Me in my mind: Dance party!

Although it may seem that empathizing with others best means carrying their burdens with or for them, loving them at the highest level involves embracing a non-reactive state of helpfulness. When Paige set aside her feelings, she realized her circumstances had a much greater purpose—to create space for her son's growth and refinement.

Zig Ziglar once said, *"Difficult roads often lead to beautiful destinations."*[44] These days, Nathan has a place of his own, a thriving career, and a girlfriend!

Remember, you are not your circumstances. You are not your behavior. You are not a victim. You get to

You get to own your perspective.

choose how to interpret all situations. You get to own your perspective. And that's a beautiful, life-changing way to live.

CHAPTER 17

GET EXCITED ABOUT
WHAT'S TO COME

"Your soul has a curious shape because it is a hollow
made to fit a particular swelling in the infinite
contours of the Divine substance."[45]

—C.S. LEWIS

Do **you get bored easily**? *Me too.* Do you crave fun and variety? *Ditto.* Do you want more than what you have? *Same here!* Do you look for what's next? *I'm scanning the horizon right there with you!*

This never-sated, *I-want-more* yearning used to perplex me. I asked myself, *Am I discontent? Unsatisfied? Not doing all I'm created for?* One day I realized that the answer to each of those questions is a resounding *yes!* And that's a good thing! My *I-want-more* yearning rises like heat from a hollow deep in my soul. It's a hollow made by the thumbprint of my God, who tells me, *Chris, this world is not your home. It's just Hotel Earth. The best is yet to come and is worth the wait!*

I love superhero movies. Give me a tale of rescue, and I'm ecstatic! I'm drawn to these stories because my God wired me to yearn for a hero who is worth the wait. As a Christian, Jesus

Christ is my hero. One day, He'll rescue me from this radically imperfect world and lift me to my ideal heaven. I can only imagine that utopia—and yet I know it's going to be life beyond my wildest dreams!

You, too, were born for a life far more fabulous than this one on Earth. You crave more because of your creator's thumbprint on your soul, which tells you life down here isn't all there is. The best is yet to come! *How's that for good news?*

Spiritual teacher Ram Dass once said, *"We're all just walking each other home,"* [46] describing how humans create a community of love on Earth as we journey to what awaits us beyond this lifetime. What's your home? Your heaven? Whatever the next life is for you, that's where your ideal exists.

Knowing that there are things you'll not see this side of your heaven isn't a bummer. Instead, it's permission to push forward toward your divine-given desires without the guilt of feeling you aren't good enough, fast enough, or smart enough. Because you are enough! Knowing this truth will help you momentarily dance with dissatisfaction—and get excited about what's to come.

You want more because your higher power created you for more.

You want more because your higher power created you for more. And you'll get there one day. Think of your yearning for something better as an incredible blessing that can change your life and those around you. Use the following exercise to celebrate and engage that belief:

What will I allow my zeal for more drive me to do with the time I have on Earth?

_____

_____

_____

How does this view of contentment (knowing that life on Earth isn't all there is) make me feel?

_____

_____

_____

How will I dance with my present circumstances, knowing they need not be perfect?

_____

_____

_____

How do I want to show up in the real world today as I anticipate an ideal world later?

_____

_____

_____

After completing this exercise, place your answers where you can often see them. They'll encourage you to stay engaged in making this world a better place even while your heart beats to the rhythm of your God-shaped yearning for the ultimate perfection to come.

FAITH FOR THE RACE

American humorist Cullen Hightower once said, *"Faith is building on what you know is here so you can reach what you know is there."*[47] Faith is fuel for the tough here and now. Without the guidance of spiritual faith, we risk exhausting ourselves to force perfection on a world that's incapable of it. The trick to living life all in is knowing that it's ok to run toward perfection; as long as we remember, we will never fully attain it this side of eternity.

Without the guidance of spiritual faith, we risk exhausting ourselves to force perfection on a world that's incapable of it.

I love the press-on wisdom found in the scriptures 1 Corinthians 9:25-26 and Philippians 3:14:

*"All athletes are disciplined in their training. They do it to win a prize
that will fade away, but we do it for an eternal prize. So I run with
purpose in every step. I am not just shadowboxing."*

*"I press on to reach the end of the race and receive the heavenly prize
for which God, through Christ Jesus, is calling us."*

Speaking of racing, I've been hitting the pavement with high-
performance running shoes for years. And I can happy-dance a
completed 5K with the best of them! I'm in my sweet spot when
sprinting toward a goal with Bon Jovi booming in my earbuds.

Yet when I strive for the ideal off the running trail and don't
attain it, I can become overwhelmed, angry, and paralyzed. And
when I cannot heap any more responsibility onto myself for not
making things perfect, I can offload that blame onto others. I can
accuse, judge, and melt into martyrdom. I risk stalling forward
movement and even giving up altogether. It isn't a pretty picture,
and I strive not to live that way! I want to run a good faith mara-
thon on Earth, stirring up progress and love instead of inefficiency
and confusion.

What is it that you want? Take heart and move forward with
assurance that, although you won't attain perfection and may not
fully see the fruits of your race on Earth, your work here is pur-
poseful and will be celebrated in the next life. You are "building
on what you know is here, so you can reach what you know is
there!" That's faith for the race.

Ask yourself these questions as you pace your race in the real
world:

How will I allow my spiritual beliefs and drive for ideal circumstances to push and pull me forward to help myself and others in real circumstances?

_____

_____

_____

Am I exhausting myself fighting for an ideal situation?

_____

_____

_____

What is a more productive way to contribute to the real change I want to experience?

_____

_____

_____

Do I love what I do, or am I searching to only do what I love?

_____

_____

_____

How will I love what I already do even more? What's great about my real life?

_____

_____

_____

As my clients answer these questions, momentum shifts. They get energized to either find more joy in their current job, relationship, community, or situation—or empowered to change their job, relationship, community, or situation. Physical change may or may not be necessary to make these changes; however, mindset thrust is a must.

When you stop fighting for perfection on Earth, you'll get resourceful and generate real heart and mindset change. That change will

You play a vital role in the wonder of tomorrow, and today is the best time to get excited about what's to come!

free you to love yourself, your relationships, work, and life. With that in mind, place your hands over that divine-shaped hollow in your heart and remember this: You play a vital role in the wonder of tomorrow, and today is the best time to get excited about what's to come!

CHAPTER 18

BELIEVE YOU HAVE
EVERYTHING

"Resilience is born by grounding yourself in
your own loveliness, hitting notes you thought
were way out of your range."[48]

—FATHER GREGORY BOYLE

You have everything you need to live all in! You have everything you need to get where you want to go. You have everything you need to ignite your resourcefulness, embrace your empowering story, and focus on the life you want.

As you move forward, you'll want to refresh yourself on your growth from time to time. (We all need refreshers and tune-ups!) Remind yourself of your magnificence quite often—because you are that and more. Make sure you also surround yourself with people who believe in you. (We all need individuals in our lives who remind us of our splendor.)

After our initial work together, most of my clients return for tune-ups one, six, or even twelve months after our final session. These sessions remind them of the incred-

Remind yourself of your magnificence quite often—because you are that and more.

ible work they accomplished and their investment in themselves. They recall their resilience and loveliness. (We all need reminders.)

Remember Dale, the architect from chapter four who changed his life by changing his story? He booked a tune-up session about six months after our initial work together. He said his job was going better than ever, his relationships continued to be meaningful, and he loved learning more about nutrition and physical wellness.

Although Dale was building a life he loved, old thought patterns had started to creep back. He noticed this happening and reached out to me for a tune-up. (Way to go, Dale!) Here's how our conversation went:

Dale: I booked this session because I've noticed my old story rearing its ugly head, especially when I'm tired and not paying attention to my thoughts.

Me: If you're not paying attention to your thoughts, how do you know your old story is rearing its head?

Dale: Because I'll be in the middle of my work day, or even doing something fun on a weekend, and I'll just feel bad for no reason. Then I realize it's because an old lousy thought was in my head.

Me: That's awesome! Celebrate yourself for that!

Dale: Huh? What for?

Me: For paying attention to your thoughts! You used your bad feeling as an alarm to get curious. You knew exactly what thought went through your head to make you feel bad. Celebrate that! You didn't have this skill when we first started working together. Remember those stories that bounced through your mind and made you feel so lousy?

Dale: Ugh. Yep. Back then, I was so unaware of my destructive thoughts.

Me: And now you are aware! You booked this session because you recognized a disempowering story. So, that's awesome!

Dale: Yeah. Ok, cool. But how do I change the resurfacing thoughts now that I know about them?

Me: If you had to answer that question for yourself, how would you answer it?

Dale: How did I know you'd ask that? Well, I think I'd get a piece of paper and write it down. That's how we did it before. I'd write it out, and then circle only what's true.

Me: Let's do that then. Tell me the last thought you noticed that made you feel bad.

Dale: Last week I was at work, starting a project with a new team. I felt terrible walking into that first meeting. I hadn't felt that way in a while, so it freaked me out, and the crappiness escalated. I started feeling anxious and incompetent, like a fraud working with experts.

Me: Great! And what was the thought going through your mind at that moment?

Dale: *I don't deserve to be here. I'm a screw up. These people are going to find out what a loser I really am.*

Me: Is that true? Are you a screw up and loser who didn't belong in that meeting?

Dale: Of course not! I've already worked through all that. That's why the thought freaked me out. I thought I was past that self-sabotaging thinking. Am I slipping back to my old story?

Me: Do you think you are?

Dale: No, I'm living my new story. Everything is going great.

Me: That's right, Dale. Because your thought in that meeting was just that, a thought. It was not and is not true. It's simply an old pattern popping back into your subconscious. It cannot hurt you unless you allow it to. You already put in the work to empower your life. You got curious enough about the thought to bring it to your conscious mind and question it. You're living your desired story. You're in control of what you believe and don't believe. And you're uber-intelligent for calling out your own lousy thought. Again, celebrate that!

You're in control of what you believe and don't believe.

Dale: So, how do I keep it from happening again?

Me: Can you keep it from happening again?

Dale: Actually, no.

Me: So, what can you control when it happens again, when you have a lousy thought or find yourself asking a lousy question?

Dale: Flip it to a better one! Circle the truth. Remember what I can control. And not freak out; it's just a thought. It can't hurt me.

Me: Brilliant! Let's keep using this example to further lock in your refreshed tools. How will you flip your realized thought, *I'm a screw up and a loser who doesn't belong in this meeting?*

Dale: I'll flip it to the truth instead. That thought is an old lie my mind created. I'm smarter than my thoughts, especially the ones that float around when I'm tired or excited about a new situation. The truth is, I deserve the job and my new team. I'm a talented architect and the perfect person for the role I'm in.

Me: Yes, Dale, you are! Say it again. This time shout it.

Dale: I deserve the job and my team! I'm a talented architect and the perfect person for the role I'm in!

Me: I love it! Based on our past coaching assignments, what do you think would be an impactful assignment for you after this session?

Dale: I'll write my new truth out and recite it as a mantra throughout the day—for sure when I wake up and before I go to bed. I'll make it my focus. This worked best for me to lock in empowering thought patterns in the past. I'll pick up this mantra ritual again.

Me: Fabulous!

Dale: I needed this tune-up to remind myself how much I already know! Thank you! Super excited about getting after it with the new team now!

Now that you've worked through *Living All In*, come back to it for tune-ups. Refresh the tools that worked best for you. Here are some questions to remind yourself of your resilience and brilliance:

What in my life feels hard at the moment?

_____

_____

_____

What difficult things have I overcome in my past?

_____

_____

_____

How did I do it?

_____

_____

_____

What parts of myself did I tap to make it happen?

_____

_____

_____

What tools did I use?

_____

_____

_____

How will I take that same resourcefulness and apply it to my current situation?

_____

_____

_____

Write down what comes to you. Then, focus on your answers instead of the problem as you move forward to the solution. Should your focus veer back to the problem, celebrate your awareness of that and immediately shift attention back to the solution to reignite your resourceful state of mind.

YOU DECIDE

We've covered a lot of ground in *Living All In*, and you get to decide what teachings stick. The bottom line? Take the wisdom that works for you and meld it into your nervous system with conditioning and repetition. Whatever you decide you want, be intentional about committing to it over time. Use what you learned in this book, and create your own meaningful methods to add to it. Choose what you want, who you want to be, and where you want to go.

> Grow to recognize and revere all your emotions because all feelings are helpful.

Grow to recognize and revere all your emotions because all feelings are helpful. They signal you to mind your mind. They alert you to go forward, sit still, or steer clear.

Your thoughts will shape your dreams or

your despair. So, choose those that embolden your dreams to come true! Your magnificent mind is your guide to showing up for the life you want.

Romans 12:2 (NIV) tells us, *"Do not conform to the pattern of this world, but be transformed by the renewing of your mind . . ."* Take that divine wisdom deep into your soul—and then live it out loud!

Here's a graduation exercise to celebrate your journey and set your mind and heart on living a life you love:

Breathe in deeply, exhale, and then say the following words aloud:

The renewing of my mind transforms me.

I am whole and ready to go.

I choose patterns, focus, and stories that sustain and grow me.

I have everything I need to show up for the life I want!

Now, go live your life all in, my friend. You are magnificent!

NOTES

1. Kinnell, Galway, *Saint Francis and the Sow: Mortal Acts, Mortal Words*, Houghton Mifflin Harcourt, Boston, MA, First Edition, 1980.
2. *https://www.azquotes.com/author/12603-Eleanor_Roosevelt*
3. Smith, James K.A. *You Are What You Love*. Brazos Press, a division of Baker Publishing Group. Grand Rapids, MI, 2016. p.2.
4. Beck, Martha, *https://www.opruh.com/spirit/how-to-figure-out-what-you-want-in-life*. Accessed April 13, 2022.
5. Max Lucado, "You Are Special," Crossway Books, a division of Good News Publishers, Wheaton, IL, 1997, p. 19.
6. Frankl, Viktor. *Man's Search for Meaning*, Boston: Beacon Press, 1959. p.66.
7. "You're the Indian Now," *Yellowstone*. Created by Taylor Sheridan, Season 3, Episode 1. Peacock, 2020.
8. J.K Rowling, Quote of Albus Dumbledore from the movie, *Harry Potter and the Deathly Hallows, Part 2 (#7)*, Warner Brothers Pictures, 2011.
9. Ibid.
10. John 8:32
11. J.K. Rowling, Quote of Albus Dumbledore from the movie *Harry Potter: The Chamber of Secrets*, Warner Brothers Pictures, 2002.
12. J.R.R. Tolkien, *The Fellowship of the Ring: The Lord of the Rings Part One* (Boston. New York: Houghton Mifflin Harcourt, 1954), page 50.
13. J. K. Rowling, Quote of Albus Dumbledore in the movie, *Harry Potter and the Prisoner of Azkaban*, Warner Brothers Pictures, 2004.
14. Cloud, Henry, *The Secret Things of God: Unlocking the Treasures Reserved for You*, Howard Books, a division of Simon & Schuster, Inc. New York, NY, 2007, p. 54.
15. Quote accredited to William Wordsworth.
16. Cloud, Henry, *The Secret Things of God: Unlocking the Treasures Reserved for You*, Howard Books, a division of Simon & Schuster, Inc. New York, NY, 2007, p. 54.
17. Young, William, *The Shack*, Newbury Park, CA: Windblown Media printed in association with Hachette Book Group USA, 2007, p.114.

18. Frankl, Viktor. *Man's Search For Meaning.* Boston: Beacon Press, 1959. p.134.

19. Henley, William Ernest, "Invictus," 1875. https://poets.org/poem/invictus. Public Domain.

20. Durant, Will. *The Story of Philosophy: The Lives and Opinions of the Great Philosophers of the Western World.* Simon & Schuster Paperbacks, New York, NY; 2nd edition. 1926, 1927, 1933, renewed 1954, 1955, 1961. First Simon & Schuster Paperback edition 2005. p.61

21. "The Powerful Lesson Maya Angelou Taught Oprah" timestamp: 2:35. Oprah's LIFECLASS. OWN: Oprah Winfrey Network, aired on 10/19/2011.

22. Joseph R. Cooke, *Celebration of Grace*, Zondervan: Grand Rapids, MI, 1990, p. 13.

23. Miller, Doug. Plum Creek Church, Castle Rock, CO. *www.plumcreek.church.* Sermon 11-21-21. "Offended: Pride and Love."

24. John C. Maxwell. Twitter post. July 9, 2021, 6 a.m. *http://twitter.com/TheJohnCMaxwell.*

25. Paulo Coelho, *Eleven Minutes*, HarperCollins, New York, New York, 2004, p. 37.

26. Kushner, Harold, *Forward to Man's Search for Meaning*, Boston: Beacon Press, 2006.

27. Holiday, Ryan, *The Obstacle Is The Way.* Penguin Group. New York, NY, 2014. p. 44.

28. Pueblo, Yung. Twitter @YungPueblo. Posted 6/26/21, *http://twitter.com/YungPueblo.*

29. Maniatis, Claudia. @oscarmaniatis, Instagram post 12-13-2021, WillStrong Foundation, 2020, *https://www.willstrongcancerfoundation.org*

30. Clifford, Steve. Westgate Church, Saratoga CA. *www.westgatechurch.org.* Sermon 2-14-2015. "Myth Conceptions Part 4: Pray and Grow Rich."

31. *https://twitter.com/paulocoelho/status/192573337921269760?lang=en April 18, 2012.*

32. Les Brown. *https://www.brainyquote.com/authors/les-brown-quotes.* Accessed March 15, 2022.

33. Lewis, C.S. "On Living In An Atomic Age." *Present Concerns: Journalistic Essays.* 1948.

34. Wooden, John. *They Call Me Coach.* Bantam Books, New York, 1973. p. 71

35. Finerman, Wendy and Tisch, Steve (Producers), & Zemeckis, Robert, (Director), 1994. *Forrest Gump* [Motion Picture]. United States: Paramount Pictures Studio.

36. Attributed to Saint Francis of Assisi.

37. Viktor Frankl, in *Man's Search for Meaning* (1946), was likely quoting Friedrich Nietzsche from his *Twilight of the idols, or How to Philosophize with a Hammer.*

38. Original format developed by George T Doran, *There's a S.M.A.R.T. Way to Write Management's Goals and Objectives.* November 1981, *Management Review,* p. 35, 36.

39. Aesop's Fables, "The Dog and the Shadow." Wordsworths Classics, Translation by V. S. Vernon Jones, 1994, London, England, p. 44.

40. Ibid.
41. Quote attributed to Rumi, Jalal al-Din Muhammad.
42. *https://www.facebook.com/StevenFurtick/posts/your-perspective-will-either -become-your-prison-or-your-passport-it-will-either-/1019263/* October 27, 2015.
43. Paul Coelho. *https://twitter.com/paulocoelho/status/1030193763778523137*
44. *https://twitter.com/thezigziglar/status/854077020132847620?lang=en*
45. C.S. Lewis, *www.cslewisinstitute.org/Reflections_The_Signature_on_Each_Soul*, taken from *The Problem of Pain*, HarperCollins Publishers, New York, New York, 1940, 1996, p. 153.
46. *https://www.ramdass.org.* Accessed March 31, 2022.
47. *https://www.brainyquote.com/quotes/cullen_hightower_152879*
48. Boyle, Gregory, *Tattoos on the Heart*, New York, NY: Free Press, A Division of Simon & Schuster, Inc., 2010, p. 94.

Made in the USA
Las Vegas, NV
19 November 2022

59790397R10109